Life Changing Revelations

By

Andries Roux

**Revelations that will transform and
Renew your mind**

Marleo Publiseerders

PO Box25611

Monumentpark

0105

First Impression 2016

Copyright :Andries Roux

Print by Jotha Drukkers

012 460 5964/083 453 0969

ISBN: 9780620621823

4

Boodskap/Message

Aan To:_______________________________

Datum/ Date:_______________________________

____

____

____

____

Handtekening/Signature

Dedications

I am dedicating this Holy Book of Revelation to God our
Father, to Jesus Christ our Savior and to Holy Spirit our Helper. Thank You God in Trinity for helping me write this book.

It could only have been written by You, Holy Spirit, giving me practical situations in my life, and experiencing struggles so I could learn lessons from it, apply it and share it in this book.

Many thanks go out to my wife and three beautiful daughters. They are just a blessing to me, and I love them so much.

To all my friends who are mentioned and partook in writing this book – you made this book a living testimony.

To you, the reader of this book – may you be as blessed in reading it as I was blessed in writing it.

Note: Remember not all will agree with the teachings and lessons in this book, but it is fine. Take what you can out of it and reject the rest.

1 Co 13:9 We know only a portion of the truth, and what we say about God is always incomplete.

1 Co 13:10 But when the Complete arrives, our incompletes will be cancelled.

Act 3:21 Whom heaven must retain until the time for the complete restoration...
I bless you all in the Mighty Name of our Lord and Savior, Jesus Christ.

Andries Roux

Table of Contents

Revelation 1
Restoration vs. Revival

There were so many revivals through the years - the healing revival, the revival of tongues, and the Holy Spirit revival. God said to me there will be **no more revivals, there will only be restoration.** Let me explain: people have a misconception about revival; people think it must be thousands of people coming to Christ.

People think the way you judge if it's a revival, is by the amount of people attending. If people are crying for revival they are actually crying that thousands must come to Christ. God is changing that conception, by saying **no revival, but restoration.**

Restoration can be one person or a thousand coming to Christ, it can be one, or a thousand people's finances, or health being restored. It is not about the amount of people attending, but about people being restored. **It's about life, health, finances, joy, and a relationship with each other and with God being stolen by the devil, being restored back, at least double.**

Job 42:10 "And the Lord turned the captivity of Job and restored his fortunes, when he prayed for his friends; also the Lord gave Job twice as much as he had before."

The dictionary explains **revival and restoration** like this:

Christianity/revival: **Evangelical** **Christian** **meeting:** A meeting, or a series of meetings, of evangelical Christians intended to awaken religious fervour in those who attend.
Restoring of something removed: the return of something that was removed or abolished.
Restoring of something to former condition: the restoring of something such as buildings or furniture to an earlier and usually better condition.
Thing **restored**: something, especially a building that has been brought back to an earlier and usually better condition

I have this desire in me to raise the dead, and a few years ago I had a dream. In the dream God said you shall not raise the dead, but you shall restore. Restoration is a more complete package than just raising the dead, revival, healing, relationships or finances. God wants not only to raise the dead, revive, heal good relations, or break us through in finances, but He wants to restore us completely. He wants to restore at least double back that the devil has stolen from us.

John 10:10 "The thief comes only in order to steal and kill and destroy. I came that they may have and enjoy life, and have it in abundance (to the full, till it overflows)."

My testimony: A rake was stolen out of my garage; I said to God, "Lord I sow this stolen rake." Two weeks later I was driving and next to the road was a box with five new rakes. God restored the rake that was stolen from me back five times.

Jesus is only coming back to a **completely restored, perfect bride**.

Our cry is: restore us God. Manifest restoration now. **Rest**oration = **Rest**, peace and trust in Jesus that He has restored us. Thank you Father for complete restoration already paid for by Jesus.

Act 3:20 "And that He may send the Christ, who before was designated and appointed for you even Jesus."

Act 3:21 "Whom heaven must receive [*and retain*] until the time for the complete restoration of all that God spoke by the mouth of all His holy prophets for ages past."

Revelation 2
Thus says the Lord: This year 2011 is the year of Restoration!!!

By the inspiration of God I started the ministry: House of
Restoration and Extreme Miracles Ministry. **God said to me**: There will never be revivals anymore. In the past there was the revival of tongues, the healing revival, the charismatic revival, the Toronto revival.
God said: Now is the time for restoration and resurrection.

Every person needs **restoration** in some or other area of his life, perhaps healing or finances or a relationship needs **restoration.**

In other cases there is no hope anymore and these people's healing, finances or relationships need to be **resurrected**.
It's like a house, we are all houses, any house needs fixing, repairing, restoring. Some houses do not need **restoration**, but need to be **resurrected**. These houses need a new foundation, a **completely resurrected** house.

Jesus will not return until all houses have been restored and resurrected, no rapture, no flyaway

rapture theology. A complete restoration of all houses, the perfect body.

It is each and every born again, Spirit filled Christian's responsibility to **restore and resurrect** each other in Christ's name. Like praying for the sick, sharing the love of Christ, giving, **restoring the body of Christ, and resurrecting the house of God through the power of the name of Jesus Christ.**

Act 3:21 "Whom heaven must receive [and retain] until the time for the **complete restoration** of all that God spoke by the mouth of all His holy prophets for ages past."

Rom 8:11 "And if the Spirit of Him Who raised up Jesus from the dead dwells in you, He Who raised up Christ Jesus from the dead will also restore to life your mortal (short-lived, perishable) bodies through His Spirit Who dwells in you."

When Jesus was crucified He went into hell and set the captives free. So the unbelievers' spirits and souls were taken out of hell by Jesus. They accepted Jesus as their Saviour and were set free.

1 Pe 3:18 "For Christ died for sins once for all, the Righteous for the unrighteous (the Just for the unjust, the Innocent for the guilty), that He might bring us to God. In His human body He was put to death, but He was made alive in the spirit."

1 Pe 3:19 "In which He went and preached to the spirits in prison."

1 Pe 3:20 "[The souls of those] who long before in the days of Noah had been disobedient, when God's patience waited during the building of the ark in which a few, actually eight in number, were saved through water."

Mat 27:52 "And the graves were opened; and many bodies of the saints which slept arose."

Mat 27:53 "And came out of the graves after his resurrection, and went into the holy city, and appeared unto many."

Ezek 37:13 "And ye shall know that I am the LORD, when I have opened your graves, O my people, and brought you up out of your graves."

My opinion: We can imitate Jesus. Why must we raise the dead? We must get the unbeliever out of hell to repent and become a believer in Christ, because Christ died for all.

1 Pe 3:18 "For Christ died for sins once for **all**, the Righteous for the unrighteous (the Just for the unjust, the Innocent for the guilty), that He might bring us to God. In His human body He was put to death, but He was made alive in the spirit."

John 3:16 "For God so greatly loved and dearly prized the world that He gave up His only Begotten Son, so that whoever believes in (trusts in, clings to, relies on) Him shall not perish (come to destruction, be lost) but have eternal (everlasting) life."

Luke 15:4 "What man of you, if he has a hundred sheep and should lose one of them, does not leave the ninety-nine in the wilderness and go after the one that is lost until he finds it?"

Say for instance a three-year old Moslem girl dies. She did not have the opportunity or time to accept Jesus as her Saviour. Her body goes to the grave; her spirit and soul go to hell. So if we can raise her body out of the grave by calling her spirit and soul out of hell back into her body, we have set her free out of hell like Jesus did. She then accepts Jesus as her Saviour.

Mat 18:14 "Just so it is not the will of My Father Who is in heaven that one of these little ones should be lost and perish."

1 Co 15:26 "The last enemy shall be destroyed *is* death."

John 5:25 "Believe Me when I assure you, most solemnly I tell you, the time is coming and is here now when the dead shall hear the voice of the Son of God and those who hear it shall live."

John 5:28 "Do not be surprised and wonder at this, for the time is coming when all those who are in the tombs shall hear His voice."

John 5:29 "And they shall come out--those who have practiced doing good to the resurrection of life, and those who have done evil will be raised for judgment."

God spoke to me, and said: I will show you I am serious and mean what I said that **this year, 2012, is the year of resurrection.** I worked for 23 days for a company that burns medical waste in a fiery furnace, incinerating this medical waste. I cried when I saw hundreds, thousands of little dead babies and aborted babies going into that fiery hell. **God said:** Pray that all these babies be **resurrected to life, pray that the captives be freed out of hell**, because I love all these dead babies. I knew them before they were born. I died to bring them life.

So when we had a shutdown at work, I climbed into that hellish furnace and anointed the inside of that furnace with oil and called every little dead baby's soul back to life.

Ps 139:13 "For You did form my inward parts; You did knit me together in my mother's womb."

Pro 30:16 "Sheol (the place of the dead), the barren womb, the earth that is not satisfied with water, and the fire that says not, It is enough."

In 2006 I had 3 dreams in succession.

.   I was in a mortuary and I said to a man: " Come, come, it's time to stand up out of the dead. He came out and was dripping with water, like he was defrosting.

•   I was in my hometown in the graveyard and a bright light came out of a grave and an old

man stood up out of the grave. Then I went to the children's graves and there also came a

light and a child stood up. A few days later I physically visited that graveyard and went to

the grave God showed me. The grave I saw in my dream was on the children side in the graveyard. The child's name on the tombstone was Jane Nell. My youngest daughter's name is Janelle.

•   Our pastor called me out in a church meeting and told me to raise the 4 people lying dead in church.

Restoration and Resurrection is an ongoing work until we reach perfection.

Phi 3:12 "Not that I have now attained [*this ideal*], or have already been made perfect, but I press on to lay hold of and make my own, that for which Christ Jesus (the Messiah) has laid hold of me and made me His own."

Heb 6:1 "Therefore leaving the principles of the doctrine of Christ, let us go on unto perfection; not laying again the foundation of repentance from dead works, and of faith toward God."

Rom 8:23 "And not only the creation, but we ourselves too, who have and enjoy the first fruits of the Spirit [*a foretaste of the blissful things to come*] groan inwardly as we wait for the redemption of our bodies [*from sensuality and the grave, which will reveal*] our adoption (our
manifestation as God's sons)."

Revelation 3
End - Time Groaning

I was listening to the news on the radio about the massive earthquake in Japan and God said to me: "Do you know why there are so many earthquakes, floods, hurricanes, snow storms, ozone layer and disasters on the earth?" It is because the earth is moaning, groaning and crying out for **the manifestation of the sons of God. What must the sons of God do? - They must restore the earth.**

Rom 8:19-23 "For creation (all nature) waits expectantly and longs earnestly for God's sons to be made known. For the creation (nature) was subjected to frailty, not because of some intentional fault on its part, but by the will of Him Who so subjected it with the hope that nature (creation) itself will be set free from its bondage to decay and corruption into the glorious freedom of God's children. We know that the whole creation has been moaning together in the pains of labor until now and not only the creation, but we ourselves too, who have and enjoy the first fruits of the Spirit groan inwardly as we wait for the redemption of our bodies, our adoption (our manifestation as God's sons)."

We see earthquakes, floods, hurricanes, snow storms and disasters in people's personal lives as well as in rapes, murders, suicides and it will increase, not **because** it's the **end of times** and doom and gloom will come as some preachers preach, but we must stand up in our responsibility as sons of God and restore and fix that which is broken.

Gal 4:7 "Therefore, you are no longer a slave (bond servant) but a son; and if a son, then an heir by the aid of God, through Christ."

We all are God's sons and we need to restore the earth and restore people's lives, because the earth is our inheritance and we need to speak deliverance to it.

Ps 37:22 "For such as are blessed of God shall [*in the end*] inherit the earth, but they that are cursed of Him shall be cut off."

Ps 37:29 "The righteous shall inherit the land and dwell upon it forever."

My opinion is that Jesus will only come when there is complete restoration in this earth and if the lives of people are completely restored, because Jesus is coming to a perfect, spotless bride.

Act 3:21 "Whom heaven must receive [*and retain*] until the time for the complete restoration of all that God spoke by the mouth of all His holy prophets for ages past."

Who are these sons of God?

Rom 8:14 "For all who are led by the Spirit of God are sons of
God."

How must we step up to our responsibility towards God to set the earth and people free from bondage? By being in tune with Holy Spirit. Jesus said I can only do what My Father tells me. In this same manner we are prompted by the Holy Spirit to say: Storm be still; I command you to take up your bed and walk; rise up out of your grave in Jesus name.

Rom 8:26-27 "So too the Spirit comes to our aid and bears us up in our weakness; for we do not know what prayer to offer, nor how to offer it worthily as we ought, but the Spirit Himself goes to meet our supplication and pleads in our behalf with unspeakable yearnings and groaning too deep for utterance. And He who searches the hearts of men knows what is in the mind of the Spirit, because the Spirit intercedes and pleads [*before God*] in behalf of the saints according to and in harmony with God's will."

All creation is subjected to us by Jesus.

Ps 8:6 "You made him to have dominion over the works of
Your hands; You have put all things under his feet:"

****

So come on, sons of God, step up to your
responsibility and bring restoration in
Jesus name!!!

Revelation 4

Are you a scavenger or a son of God?

A while ago God spoke to me through a cat. We got a small kitten for my youngest daughter and in the process of this cat growing up; I looked closely to what she was doing. She always walked across the kitchen floor looking for food and little scraps falling off the table. While observing her for a few days doing this, God dropped these words into my spirit. **You are not a scavenger; you are a son!!!!**

Immediately I understood, God wants us to have more than enough, but we are like scavengers looking for pity. We sweep the ground for scraps falling from the master's table while we should be dining with the master.

On another occasion God spoke to me again. A few friends and I went to a mining equipment show.

At the show there were a lot of stalls showing people the newest equipment and products on the market and each stall had free gifts like pens, books, food, drinks, etc. So my friends I started talking to these exhibitors and went from stall to stall, just scavenging for the free gifts and God said to me: **You are not a scavenger you are a son!!!!**

Immediately I stopped scavenging and manipulating the exhibitors for gifts.

One of my friends was still busy talking and scavenging at this one stall. I then went and sat on a chair watching this scene in front of me, not talking to anybody. After a while this exhibitor came to me and offered me a cool drink. Then God spoke again to me and said: "You see, if you are a son, blessings will come to you, you don't have to scavenge or manipulate people to get what you want.

**My question to you is:
Are you a scavenger or a son of God?**

Revelation 5
Labelling &
judgments!!!
What does your
label say?

When I was still a child and did not clean my room or do chores around the house, my mother used to say that I was a lazy boy. I carried this label for many years, but last night I heard someone said: „Pull off the judgments and labels people put on you". This statement really touched me.

I went into our living room and prayed to our Father as Holy

Spirit led me. I prayed: „In Jesus name, I pull off every **label and judgment** that was put on me by my mother and other people, knowingly or unknowingly. As I was praying, I saw that I had my t-shirt on inside out and the label of the t-shirt was in front, under my chin, nearly in my mouth. So I pulled it off and said: „In Jesus name, no one will ever label me as lazy or any other bad thing anymore. I label myself now the blessed of God. I label myself successful, excellent, prosperous, healthy and wealthy in Jesus name. „ **What you say is what you get!!!**

Pro 18:20 "A man's self shall be filled with the fruit of his mouth; and with the consequence of his words he must be satisfied."

Pro 18:21 "Death and life are in the power of the tongue, and they who indulge in it shall eat the fruit of it."

Labels and judgments initiated by the devil come in 2 forms. Through you and through people, but the bible says Jesus did not come to judge, but to save and that we should not even judge ourselves.
Joh 3:17 "For God did not send the Son into the world in order to judge (to reject, to condemn, to pass sentence on) the world but that the world might find salvation and be made safe and sound through Him."

1 Co 4:3 "But it matters very little to me that I should be put on trial by you and that you or any other human tribunal should investigate and question and cross-question me. I do not even put myself on trial and judge myself."

Two months ago my wife came to me and said that this one person talked badly about me. I totally lost my peace, because it was not the truth. I called this person and said with authority that she had to come to my house and apologize to me. She came, stood on her knees in front of me and said: „Andries, before God I ask forgiveness for what I said"

The Bible says we shall judge the world. What does this mean? My opinion is that we shall not judge the person, but the wrong actions, not the sinner, but the sin itself.

1 Co 6:2 "Do you not know that the saints (the believers) will judge and govern the world? And if the world is to be judged and ruled by you, are you unworthy and incompetent to try of the smallest courts of justice?"

1 Co 6:3 "Do you not know also that we are to judge the angels and pronounce opinion between right and wrong? How much more then matters pertaining to this world and of this life only!"

Don't let people **label or judge** you badly, and don't judge yourself.

Ps 139:13 "Oh yes, you shaped me first inside, then out; you

formed me in my mother's womb."

Ps 139:14 "I thank you, High God--you're breathe-taking! Body and soul, I am marvellously made! I worship in adoration-what a creation!"

Ps 139:15 "You know me inside and out, you know every bone in my body; you know exactly how I was made, bit by bit, how I was sculpted from nothing into something."

Ps 139:16 "Like an open book, you watched me grow from conception to birth; all the stages of my life were spread out before you, the days of my life all prepared before I'd even lived one day."

Ps 139:17 "Your thoughts--how rare, how beautiful! God, I'll never comprehend them!" God **labels** you as successful and excellent, a son of ALL MIGHTY GOD.

Revelation 6
Enjoy life

Neh 8:10 The joy of the Lord is my strength.

The enjoyment of the Lord is my strength.

God spoke to me and I want to share this with as many people as possible. He said start enjoying life. I once worked on a diamond mine and hated it. I always said to my family I am only doing this for the money. Then my daughter Sune came to me and told me I was doing this job for the wrong reasons. She said: „Dad ask God what you can do for Him on the diamond mine."
My whole attitude changed.
I started praying for people and there came a lot of changes, just by changing my attitude, and looking for something I enjoyed.

When you are faced with any situation in life that you don't enjoy, ask God to show you something in it that is enjoyable. **For example** I want to lose weight, but I hate doing cardio and gym work, but I enjoy feeling my muscles pumped up, I enjoy feeling my muscles have been working the next morning. I hate being on a diet, but I love eating healthy foods and not feeling bloated. So when you don't see results on the scale yet, go for the enjoyment of that task, not the performance of the task, then the results follow, because my trust is not in the exercise or diet I do, but in the enjoyment of the task. This enjoyment of the task takes me out of the law of doing stuff to get results. This enjoyment gives me peace, trust and joy in God and eventually the result of enjoyment gives me breakthrough in that area.

My results and progress are not determined by me performing the task, because that is law. My results and progress are determined by my enjoyment, peace and trust in God.
You might say there is no joy in being sick, but there is joy in knowing that God is the healer and my results in getting healed flow out of my joy, peace and trust in God that He has healed. You might say there is no joy in not having money to provide, but there is joy in knowing that no matter what comes, He will never leave or forsake me, His name is Jehovah-Jireh -"The
Lord Provides."

To sum it up: Change your focus from your situation and focus on enjoying God.

Revelation 7
Lord, what is my purpose in life?

We all need purpose in life. Why are we here? What must we do? In 2008 I was at a very low point in my life with no direction or purpose. I remember as a young boy I really had no dream of being something like a doctor, lawyer or anything else and this really brought me down in 2008. I told myself I was worth nothing. I did not even have a dream of becoming something as a child.

I was praying, talking, pleading and screaming to God: **"Lord, what is my purpose in life?" What do you want me to do?**
Time and time again when I prayed this prayer God told me:" **Your purpose in life is to know me and if you know me, you can trust Me and if you trust Me, you really know Me"**

I saw a movie once about Eddie Murphy – Coming back to America. It was about this rich prince coming to America. He wanted no one to know his background. He started working in a hamburger joint and stayed in the poor part of town. He met this wonderful girl. They fell in love. She did not know he was a rich prince. Eventually he said he was a rich prince, they got married and she became a princess.

She has fallen in love with him for who he is and not for what he has.

That is what happens with our relationship with God. We want stuff from God. We are not receiving it because we want Him to only give and He wants a relationship with us. We don't want to know Him for who He is but for what He can give. That is why we sometimes don't receive from God.

It's about a relationship.

God said: **It's in knowing Me, that is where your purpose is hidden.** God said: Know Me for who I am not for what I can do or give you. God said: Your **purpose in life** is to know Me, if you know Me you can trust Me. God said: **In knowing Me is everything**, health, wealth, peace, happiness, love, etc.

After 2 years He opened up my purpose for me, to restore people. I then started this website: houseofrestoration.co.za

It's in God that your purpose is hidden. Start knowing and trusting God, your whole situation and life will change.

Phi 3:8 "Yes, furthermore, I count everything as loss compared to the possession of the priceless privilege (the overwhelming preciousness, the surpassing worth, and supreme advantage) of **knowing Christ Jesus my Lord** and of progressively becoming more deeply and intimately acquainted with Him. For His sake I have lost everything and consider it all to be mere rubbish, in order that I may win Christ."

Phi 3:9 "And that I may be found and **known as in Him**…"

Phi 3:10 "[For my determined purpose is] that I may **know Him** [that I may progressively become more deeply and intimately acquainted with Him, perceiving and recognizing and understanding the wonders of His Person more strongly and more clearly], and that I may, in that same way come to **know the power** out flowing from His resurrection, and that I may so share His sufferings as to be continually transformed to His death.

Joh 17:3 "And this is eternal life: **to know (to perceive, recognize, become acquainted with, and understand) You**, the only true and real God, and to **know Him, Jesus Christ**…"

Jer 24:7 "And I will give them a heart **to know (recognize, understand, and be acquainted with) Me,** that I am the Lord; and they will be My people, and I will be their God, for they will return to Me with their whole heart."

Quote by someone:
The greatest hunger in life is the hunger for meaning and Purpose ... If you don't find it, you'll stay hungry forever.

Revelation 8
Reminding God of his promises, reminding people of their promises and commitments

God said: If you can remind Me of My promises towards you, you can remind people of their promises and commitments towards you.

Isa 62:6-7 "I have set watchmen upon your walls, O Jerusalem, who will never hold their peace day or night; you who put the Lord in remembrance [*of His promises*], keep not silence, and give Him no rest until He establishes Jerusalem and makes her a praise in the earth."

A friend of mine Nico was waiting for an insurance policy to be paid out to him. Every time he saw me, he said he wanted to buy me a car. He said God told him to buy me a car. Every time I saw him I said, make sure it's God speaking to you, you have no obligation towards me, but if God told you to do it then you must do it. Then that seed you sow will be fruitful. So the day came and his policy was paid out.

My friend stopped talking about buying me a car. Then God told me to remind him of his promise towards me. I told the

Lord I couldn't do that. God said why? You can remind Me of My promises, you can remind him as well of his promises. So one day God opened the way for me to do it. I saw a car and texted my friend about the car. **I said: "I saw a car. If you still want to buy me a car, you can buy it, but if you cannot buy me a car anymore just tell me and know that I love you and you are free."** My friend kept his promise towards me and he bought me a car. Thank you, Jesus.

My motto in life is:
I never ask any man for money. If I need money I go to my heavenly Father and He speaks to someone's heart. If someone makes me a promise and tells me I want to give you money, I tell him make sure it's from God. If so, know I will hold you accountable on that promise. If that person cannot keep his promise towards me, I set him free in Jesus name.

This motto counts for me too. If I promise someone money, I am accountable for that promise.
We must be people of a Godly character who are accountable.

Note:
1.   I never sow to anybody if Holy Spirit does not tell me to. If He says sow, I sow and know that the ground is fruitful.
2.   Check your heart to never manipulate people to give money to you, rather go to your Heavenly Father and ask Him. Remember you are not a scavenger; you are one of God's sons.

Jer 17:5-9 "Thus says the Lord: Cursed [*with great evil*] is the strong man who trusts in and relies on frail man, making weak [*human*] flesh his arm, and whose mind and heart turn aside from the Lord."

Revelation 9
Faith and Belief = Trust

Yesterday my 8 year old daughter Janelle came to me saying:

„Dad, I sow all my money into your life now." It was a handful of coins. „Dad, agree with me now in prayer", she said. „Jesus I ask you now that you will send someone tomorrow to our front door and that, that person will give us some money". Reluctantly I agreed with her.

Today there was a knock at my front door. It was a friend of mine, Christo. He said:" Here is some money, bless you", and he went. Wow! Is God not awesome? God provided money and answered the prayer of an 8 year old child, because she **trusted** that God would provide and it happened.
A while ago I said to God that I did not understand the words faith and belief. They are too big for my understanding. God told me to go to the bible and replace these words with one word that I can understand - **trust.**

The whole Christian walk comes down to one thing: **Do you trust God or not? Trust** works like this: say for instance, I tell you I will pick you up at 11 o'clock and I am your friend, you will **trust** me and I will then pick you up at 11 o'clock, but if you do not **trust** me, you will, just in case, make other arrangements to be picked up at 11 o'clock. This works the same with

God. God, please give me a job, money or healing, God!!! No, I don't think it will happen. I don't **trust** you Jesus - I would rather worry, not **trusting** God and make other arrangements. So the problem is not that God is not caring or listening or wanting to help. It is because we do not **trust** Him and we make our own plans.

I think the biggest reason we don't receive from God is because we don't **trust** Him. We fear and are depressed, saying what's going to happen? You can check your **trust** level by checking first your fear level. **Fear = no trust in God** Here are some examples of the word faith and belief replaced by the word **trust.**

Ps 56:3 "What time I am afraid, I will have confidence in and put my **[TRUST]** and reliance in You."

Ps 56:4 "By God I will praise His word; on God I lean, rely, and confidently put my **[TRUST]**; I will not fear. What can man, who is flesh, do to me?"

Heb 11:6 "But without faith **[TRUST]** it is impossible to please and be satisfactory to Him. For whoever would come near to God must believe **[TRUST]** that God exists and that He is the rewarder of those who earnestly and diligently seek Him."

Jam 2:17 "So also faith **[TRUST],** if it does not have works (deeds and actions of obedience to back it up), by itself is destitute of power (inoperative, dead)."

Jam 2:18 "But someone will say, you have faith **[TRUST]**, and I have works. Now you show me your faith **[TRUST]** apart from any works and I by works will show you my faith."

Jam 5:15 "And the prayer of faith **[TRUST]** shall save the sick, and the Lord shall raise him up; and if he have committed sins, they shall be forgiven him."

Joh 6:29 "Jesus replied, This is the work (service) that God asks of you: that you believe **[TRUST]** in the One Whom He has sent"

Jer 17:5 "Thus says the Lord: Cursed is the strong man who **[TRUST]** in and relies on frail man, making weak flesh his arm, and whose mind and heart turn aside from the Lord."

Jer 17:7 "blessed is the man who believes in, **[TRUST]** in, and relies on the Lord, and whose hope and confidence the Lord is."

1 Ti 6:12 "Fight the good fight of the faith **[TRUST]**; lay hold of the eternal life to which you were summoned and you confessed the good confession before many witnesses."

Revelation 10
Unless the word of God becomes flesh, it will just stay a word or words

The Holy Spirit spoke to me and said: "Unless the Word of God becomes flesh, it will just stay a word or words and will not become reality and manifest into a testimony."

God spoke a word and that word became a man/flesh

Gen 1:26 "God said, let Us make mankind in Our image, after Our likeness, and let them have complete authority over the fish of the sea, the birds of the air, the beasts, and over all of the earth, and over everything that creeps upon the earth."

We must become God's Word or Words
These Words of God/we must become flesh for these Words to become reality.

****

The Word of God = Jesus in the flesh.

Joh 1:1 "In the beginning was the Word, and the Word was with God, and the Word was God Himself."

Joh 1:14 "And the Word became flesh and tabernacle among us; and we saw His glory."

Jesus in the flesh = Light of the world.

Joh 1:4 "In Him was Life, and the Life was the Light of men." **Joh 1:9** "There it was--the true Light coming into the world that illumines every person."

Jesus is not the Light of the world anymore. We are the Light of the world, Jesus the light in us.

Mat 5:14 "You are the light of the world. A city set on a hill cannot be hidden."

Now the Word/Jesus dies and springs up in many "Words/We"

Joh 12:24 "I assure you, most solemnly I tell you, unless a grain of wheat falls into the earth and dies, it remains by itself alone. But if it dies, it produces many others and yields a rich harvest."

The Word/Jesus and Holy Spirit started moving in power and miracles started happening. When Jesus/The Word was baptized and Holy Spirit moved upon Him, His ministry started.

Joh 1:32 "John gave further evidence, saying, I have seen the Spirit descending as a dove out of heaven, and it dwelt on
Him."

Joh 1:33 "And I did not know Him nor recognize Him, but He Who sent me to baptize in water said to me, Upon Him Whom you shall see the Spirit descend and remain, that One is He Who baptizes with the Holy Spirit."

Joh 1:3 "And I have seen and my testimony is that this is the
Son of God!"

Jesus' words He spoke became flesh

Jesus, the Word of God, His words became flesh/reality when He said: "I am the Resurrection and the Life." These **words** became flesh and reality with the crucifixion and resurrection.
Unless those **words** HE spoke became flesh/reality through **action**, they would just have stayed words. They would not have manifested. Not until **His words** became a testimony.

Jesus spoke words and those words manifested in a healing.

Mat 8:16 "When the evening was come, they brought unto him many that were possessed with devils: and he cast out the spirits with *his* word and healed all that were sick."

Luke 7:7 "Wherefore neither thought I myself worthy to come unto thee: but say in a word, and My servant shall be healed."

Ps 107:20 "He sent his word, and healed them, and delivered *them* from their destructions."

****

Are we not supposed to become the words of God in flesh, moving with Holy Spirit in power?

Example - 1: We say the **Bible/The Word of God** is our guide to life, our **instruction manual**. If you buy a **TV** you read the **instruction manual** and then you use the **TV**. You do not read the **instruction manual** again and again to get more knowledge. If you do, you do not understand and know the workings of the **TV**. Only sometimes you just correct yourself quickly at the troubleshooting and recognize and rectify any mistake. You now become the **instruction manual/The Bible/The Word** and the **TV becomes Holy Spirit. It's when you don't know the TV/Holy Spirit that you have to use the instruction manual/Bible/The Word of God.**

Note: I do not see Jesus reading **The Bible/instruction manual** to get more knowledge and understanding. He just used the **Holy Spirit/TV. Jesus is the Word of God and spoke words inspired by Holy Spirit which manifested results.**

Example - 2: You can hear sermon after sermon in church. You find people going to church year after year, hearing we must **"love one another"**, but they are not acting out „**love one another'** the rest of the week. **But** if that person starts acting on those **words** by the promptings of Holy Spirit, that person becomes the **words "love one another"**. He then is **"love one another"** and does not have to hear those **words "love one another"** any more.
If someone gives you his **word and promises** you to do something, but not until that person is true to his **word** and do his **word** that he **promises** it will stay an empty **word.**

Not unless the **Word of God becomes flesh in us through reality, action and overflowing in a testimony**; it will just stay a **word or words** and will not become reality.

We must become doers and actors of the Word to become the Words of God.

Jam 1:22 "But be doers of the Word, and not merely listeners to it, betraying yourselves."

Jam 1:23 "For if anyone only listens to the Word without obeying it and being a doer of it, he is like a man who looks carefully at his natural face in a mirror."

Example - 3: If you prophesy a **word** of knowledge over a person **inspired by Holy Spirit**, is that **word** you prophesy not also the **word of God? If in your own words** you say **"God heals you" instructed by Holy Spirit, is it not exactly the same meaning as it stands in Isa 53:5 "…and with His stripes we are healed and made whole."** Are those **words** you spoke not the **word of God**? Yes. The **words** you spoke were inspired and given by the Holy Spirit and they are the **Word of God**.

Holy Spirit gave those **words** that came out of your mouth so those **words** then become **The word of God/Bible**.

2 Pe 1:21 "For the prophecy came not in old time by the will of man: but holy men of God spoke *as they were* moved by the Holy Ghost."

Example - 4: Brother Paul wrote all these beautiful letters to the Churches **inspired and helped by Holy Spirit.** These letters are now recorded in **The Bible** and are called **The Word of God**. In the same manner, if our **Words** are **inspired by Holy Spirit**, they must become **The Word of God/The Bible.**

2 Pe 1:21 "For no prophecy ever originated because some man willed it, but men spoke from God who were born along

(moved and impelled) by the Holy Spirit."

Job 26:4 "With whose assistance have you uttered these words? And whose spirit came forth from you?" **Why did we receive Holy Spirit [Acts 1:8/2:17]?We /the words of God must move with the Holy Spirit in power just like Jesus did. The Holy Spirit is the helper of the words/us.**

Joh 14:26 "But the Comforter (Counsellor, Helper, Intercessor, Advocate, Strengthener, Standby), the Holy Spirit, Whom the

Father will send in My name [*in My place, to represent*

Me and act on My behalf], He will teach you all things. And

He will cause you to recall everything I have told you."

The Word- Jesus Christ - came to save us. [Matt 18:11]
The Holy Spirit came to teach and help us/the words of
God by his promptings
[Act 1:8/21:4/Luke 2:27/Joh 14:26/Rom 8:13].

My personal opinion: We, the sons of God, **are not there yet,** but we must come to a place of perfection where **reading the Bible** is not needed anymore. We must become and live **the Bible/the words of God**, moving with the Holy Spirit in power. Every word we speak must be **inspired/instructed by the Holy Spirit,** for these **words** to become **the words of God/Bible. I don't read Bible more than 1 hour a week, but I don't go more than 5 minutes without mediating what the Holy Spirit is speaking. I don't pray more than 5 minutes a day but I don't go 5 minutes without praying, speaking and worshipping God.**

Joh 5:38 "And you have not His word living in your hearts, because you do not believe and adhere to and trust in and rely
on Him Whom He has sent."

Joh 5:39 "You search and investigate and pore over the Scriptures diligently, because you suppose and trust that you have eternal life through them. And these [*very Scriptures*] testify about Me!"

Joh 5:40 "And still you are not willing to come to Me, so that you might have life."

Revelation 11
In the sweat of your face shall you eat your bread

On 29 May 2012 I lost my job and was asked to leave the company. Our work relationship deteriorated because of me standing up against unfairness in the company, not fearing to lose my job and provision. Now I had no job or any means to provide for the future of my family. **God said to me:**

"You don't have to sweat to receive your bread and provide for yourself and your family, like Adam and Eve had to. Jesus broke the curse on the cross. You are now free to receive provision from Me. **There is only one condition: You have to trust Me as your provider.**"

Gen 3:17 "And to Adam He said, Because you have listened and given heed to the voice of your wife and have eaten of the tree of which I commanded you, saying, You shall not eat of it, the ground is under a curse because of you; in sorrow and toil shall you eat of it all the days of your life."

Gen 3:19 "In the sweat of your face shall you eat bread until you return to the ground, for out of it you were taken; for dust you are and to dust you shall return."

Gen 3:19 "... sweating in the fields from dawn to dusk, Until you return to that ground yourself, dead and buried; you started out as dirt, you'll end up dirt."

This does not mean that you don't have to work. Adam worked in the Garden; he attended to the Garden and gave names to the animals, etc. His work was his passion and purpose in life. That's what God created Adam for.

Gen 2:15 "and the Lord God took the man and put him in the
Garden of Eden to tend and guard and keep it."

Gen 2:20 "And Adam gave names to all the livestock and to the birds of the air and to every [wild] beast of the field; but for Adam there was not found a helper meet (suitable, adapted, complementary) for him."

I came to realize God is a very jealous God and does not want us to rely on and trust in our jobs or business to provide, but to only trust Him as the Provider, and when you do that, there is freedom from receiving provision in sweat. God wants to provide in abundance for us.

Exo 34:14 "For you shall worship no other god; for the Lord,
Whose name is Jealous, is a jealous God."

Phi 4:19 "And my God will liberally supply your every need according to His riches in glory in Christ Jesus."

Jer 17:5 "Thus says the Lord: Cursed is the strong man who trusts in and relies on frail man, making weak [human] flesh his arm, and whose mind and heart turn aside from the Lord."

Jer 17:7 "Blessed is the man who believes in, trusts in, and relies on the Lord, and whose hope and confidence the Lord is."

Jer 17:8 "For he shall be like a tree planted by the waters that spreads out its roots by the river; and it shall not see and fear when heat comes; but its leaf shall be green. It shall not be anxious and full of care in the year of drought, nor shall it cease yielding fruit."

God wants us to seek His kingdom first. God wants us to stand up for righteousness and to not be afraid when we lose our security to provide through worldly sources, but to trust Him as Provider. If we trust him as the Provider, then the things that the world seeks will be added to us freely, but only if we trust Him as our Provider.

Mat 6:25 "Therefore I tell you, stop being perpetually uneasy (anxious and worried) about your life, what you shall eat or what you shall drink; or about your body, what you shall put on. Is not life greater than food and the body than clothing?"

Mat 6:26 "Look at the birds of the air; they neither sow nor reap nor gather into barns, and yet your heavenly Father keeps feeding them. Are you not worth much more than they?"

Mat 6:28 "And why should you be anxious about clothes? Consider the lilies of the field and learn thoroughly how they grow; they neither toil nor spin."

We hate our jobs, but we are too afraid to step out and trust God. God is our source of provision. When we trust Him to provide, then we can do what God called us for; we can fulfil our purpose in life. We cannot serve two masters. I am not saying you should quit your job; I am saying be led by the Holy Spirit and start trusting God to be your provider. **He is Jehovah Jirah, The Lord our provider.**

Mat 6:24 "No one can serve two masters; for either he will hate the one and love the other, or he will stand by and be devoted to the one and despise and be against the other. You cannot serve God and mammon."

Mat 6:31 "Therefore do not worry and be anxious, saying, what are we going to have to eat? Or, what are we going to have to drink? Or, what are we going to have to wear?"

Mat 6:32 "For the Gentiles (heathen) wish for and crave and diligently seek all these things, and your heavenly Father knows well that you need them all."

Mat 6:33 "But seek (aim at and strive after) first of all His kingdom and His righteousness (His way of doing and being right), and then all these things taken together will be given you besides."

Mat 6:34 "So do not worry or be anxious about tomorrow, for tomorrow will have worries and anxieties of its own. Sufficient for each day is its own trouble."

Two weeks later I received THREE prophesies:

1. A pastor prophesied: There were people who hurt you, but God will compensate you, because you stood up and were not afraid to lose your provision. He already has a plan and a path for you. This will be a ridiculous miracle and the income will be just as ridiculous.
2. My friend Egbert prophesied: I see spiral steps into heaven, an open heaven.
3. An old lady prophesied: I see you like Moses with a staff in your hand, leading the way.

Since I lost my job I have experienced so much freedom, I realized I do not have security and provision for myself. I can just **trust God as my Provider.**

I started sowing money again with no fear as I used to {you reap what you sow}. I joined an online business that provides in ridiculous ways of income and money just started to flow in.

Luk 6:38 "Give, and it shall be given unto you; good measure, pressed down, and shaken together, and running over, shall men give into your bosom. For with the same measure that ye mete withal it shall be measured to you again."

Heb 13:7 "Remember your leaders and superiors in authority who brought to you the Word of God. Observe attentively and consider their manner of living and imitate their faith (their conviction that God exists and is the Creator and Ruler of all things, the Provider and Bestower of eternal salvation through Christ, and their leaning of the entire human personality on God in absolute trust and confidence in His power, wisdom, and goodness)."

People always say there is no such thing as getting rich quickly.

My opinion: I totally disagree, why can't we get rich quickly? I think it will start manifesting as soon as you start **trusting God as your Provider.** The Israelites were poor, the next day they became rich, they cleaned out the Egyptians of all their riches. **The getting rich quick scheme was initiated by God.**

Exo 3:21 And I will give this people favor and respect in the sight of the Egyptians; and it shall be that when you go, you shall not go empty-handed.

Exo 3:22 But every woman shall [*insistently*] solicit of her neighbor and of her that may be residing at her house jewels and articles of silver and gold, and garments, which you shall put on your sons and daughters; and you shall strip the Egyptians.

Quote by someone
The greatest hunger in life is the hunger for meaning and Purpose ... If you don't find it, you'll stay hungry forever.

Revelation 12
Financial healing, breakthroughs by Faith and Trust or surviving by Grace.
You choose!!!

The other day I spoke to God and asked: Lord, teach me how to get financial abundance to manifest in my house.

On **1 February** I prayed and asked: God I need $1300 to pay my debt and electricity bill by **10 February**, please provide it in Jesus name. God immediately told me to sow $130 and give it to **Cobus Jansen,** a friend of mine. At 23h00 that night I drove to the auto bank and withdrew the $130.

On **2 February** 06h00 my friend **Cobus Jansen** prayed: Lord I remind You of Your promises, You said You are my provider. I need $130 to pay my debt. I thank You Lord that You have heard my prayer; I thank You that You will provide because You promised. That morning at 07h30 he received his $130.

God already answered his prayer of **faith and trust** before he prayed that morning. **Cobus' prayer was answered by his faith and trust in God not by grace.**

Jam 1:6 "Only it must be in faith that he asks with no wavering (no hesitating, no doubting). For the one who wavers (hesitates, doubts) is like the billowing surge out at sea that is blown hither and thither and tossed by the wind."

Heb 11:6 "But without faith it is impossible to please and be satisfactory to Him. For whoever would come near to God must believe that God exists and that He is the rewarder of those who earnestly and diligently seek Him."

On **10 February** my wife told me that the crosses she was selling will bring in $1300.

On **21 February** $285 unexpectedly came in from taxes overcharged.

On **23 February** $1030 came from a total unexpected source.

We don't need grace for breakthrough. We need faith and trust in God.

Jesus and the disciples were on a boat, Jesus was sleeping. There was a big storm, the disciples were afraid and did not trust Jesus that while He was sleeping they will not drown. They woke Him to quiet the storm, **and by grace they survived the storm and came through and were saved by Jesus quieting the storm.**

If they had faith and trust in Jesus, they would have said:

"Storm be still in Jesus name".

Luk 8:24 "They woke Jesus: "Master, Master, we're going to drown!" Getting to his feet, he told the wind, "Silence!" and the waves, "Quiet down!". They did it. The lake became smooth as glass."

Luk 8:25 "Then he said to his disciples, "Why can't you trust me?" They were in absolute awe, staggered and stammering, "Who is this, anyway? He calls out to the winds and sea, and they do what he tells them!""

You can say: **grace, grace to your mountain** or you can say **mountain be removed. You choose to move in faith and trust or in grace.**
Zec 4:7 "For who are you, O great **mountain** [*of human obstacles*]? Before Zerubbabel you shall become a plain and he shall bring forth the finishing gable stone with loud shouting of the people, crying, **Grace, grace** to it!"

Mat 17:20 "And Jesus said to them, Because of your unbelief. For truly I say to you, if you have faith like a grain of mustard seed, you shall say to this **mountain**, Move from here to there. And it shall move. And nothing shall be impossible to you."

If you pray: God provide me with money to pay my bills or to heal my sickness and you worry, then the grace, unmerited favor of God will let you just, just slide through and survive that month or you will partly receive your healing.

When we ask in prayer for a need with doubt and unbelief in our hearts, the **grace, unmerited favor will pull us through. But just part of the need will be met.**

When we ask for provision or healing in prayer we must have faith and trust to receive. We **must release the outcome of the prayer and reject all fear. {Very important, discussed in: Releasing, surrendering your need in prayer, stop fighting to manifest a favourable outcome}**

Jam 1:6 "Only it must be in faith that he asks with no wavering (no hesitating, no doubting). For the one who wavers (hesitates, doubts) is like the billowing surge out at sea that is blown hither and thither and tossed by the wind."

Jam 1:7 "For truly, let not such a person imagine that he will receive anything [*he asks for*] from the Lord."

Ps 23:1 "A David psalm. GOD, my shepherd! I don't **need** a thing."

Mat 21:22 "And whatever you ask for in prayer, having faith and believing, you will receive."

People always say: By grace I was healed or by grace I prayed for provision and all my bills were paid this month, it's true but, **we ought to say:** By faith in God I am never sick or by faith in God I have more than enough finances because I have faith and trust in

God's promises when He says: You are healed and life and that in abundance.

Grace lets you just make it.
Faith and trust let you receive breakthrough.
Grace works with your unbelief.
Faith works with total peace, faith and trust in God's promises.

Eph 2:8 "Saving is all his idea, and all his work. All we do is trust him enough to let him do it. It's God's gift from start to finish!"

Heb 4:2 "For unto us was the gospel preached, as well as unto them: but the word preached did not profit them; not being mixed with faith in them that heard *it*."
My opinion: We need faith and trust not grace for breakthrough. We ought to work the works of faith, not the works of grace.

Change your speech from saying: By the grace of God we shall do this or accomplish that to saying: By faith in God we shall do this or accomplish that.

2 Ti 4:7 "I have fought the good fight, I have finished the race, I have kept the faith."
Jam 2:17 "So also faith, if it does not have works (deeds and actions of obedience to back it up), by itself is destitute of power (inoperative, dead)."

Jam 2:14 "What is the use, my brethren, for anyone to profess to have faith if he has no works? Can faith save?"

Jam 2:26 "For as the human body apart from the spirit is lifeless, so faith apart from works of obedience is also dead."

God gave us faith as a Gift. This Gift came by Grace.

Rom 4:16 "Therefore *it is* of faith so that *it might be* according to grace; for the promise to be made sure to all the seed, not only to that which is of the Law, but to that also which is of faith of Abraham, who is the father of us all."

Eph 2:8 "For it is by free grace (God's unmerited favor) that you are saved (delivered from judgment and made partakers of Christ's salvation) through faith. And this is not of yourselves, but it is the gift of God."

Revelation 13
I suggest you sow a seed, Gautam Narzary!!!

A friend of mine, Gautam, from India, sent me the following prayer request by e-mail:

Dear Brother Andries, thank for your prayer. Right now I am in need very urgently one laptop and one keyboard (Yamaha) do kindly inform your friends for the help.
Note: This is not for me but for God.

Thank
Yours truly Bro, Gautam

I e-mailed him back, saying:

Gautam my brother, I suggest you sow a seed as the Holy Spirit leads you, to harvest your laptop and keyboard.

So I challenged Gautam to sow a seed for his needs and I will sow a seed for my needs.

On the 17th of July 2011, my family and I prayed the following:

- Father, we as a family ask that you will provide us with an easy opportunity that will fit us like a glove, that will bring in billions so that we can be debt free, financially free and that this overflow of money can flow to us and other people in need.
- Father, I ask You for $7000 for the December holidays, to treat my family. Now Satan, I command you to keep your hands off my money and I command you to pay back that what you have stolen from me in Jesus" name. Angels, open doors and opportunities so that billions can flow in, in Jesus' name. I thank You now my Father. We will have peace and trust in You that this will manifest before 30 November. Amen.

The Holy Spirit suggested that I sow a seed. I only had $420, which I had made on a previous project. I actually needed this money to pay accounts, but with faith and no fear in my heart I sowed it in Jesus' name.

- I sowed $142 to Aunt Petro to buy her some new clothes.
- I sowed $57 to Deon, a friend of mine, who was in a terrible financial state.
- I sowed $57 to James, a friend of mine, who was also in a terrible financial state.
- I sowed $164 to my 3 daughters, Sune, Carla, Janelle and my wife.

The days, weeks and months passed and I went through some tough times questioning myself. Have I heard right to sow that money? During this time the devil tried many times to steal my faith and trust in God, but Jesus prayed for me so that my faith should not fail and the Holy Spirit comforted me with the word to be patient.

Luke 22:32 "But I have prayed especially for you, that your may not fail; and when you yourself have turned again, strengthen and establish your brethren."
The results of the seed sown:
- In October unexpectedly, a contract came through for my wife giving her $1928.
- On 17 November unexpectedly, a contract came through for me giving me $1142.
- On 24 November a friend of mine, Hannes, introduced me to an internet program; I invested $ 1138 giving me massive returns that already brings in money. On 31 December I have already earned $ 1160. This is exactly what I prayed for: **By sharing this opportunity, overflow money can flow to us and other people in need.**
- On 30 November a friend of mine from England, Richard Fox, blessed me with $225.

Sowed $420 - Reaped $4455+ internet business program.

God never gives you what you ask for. He always gives you more.

Eph 3:20 "Now to Him Who, by the power that is at work within us, is able to do superabundantly, far over and above all that we ask or think."

Jesus suggested to Father God that He will sow His life in order to save humanity. God then sowed His Son and it hurt Him to do it but He did it anyway. Now He reaps many sons.

John 12:24 "I assure you, most solemnly I tell you, unless a grain of wheat falls into the earth and dies, it remains by itself alone. But if it dies, it produces many others and yields a rich harvest."

I am telling you, and giving you good advice, start sowing a seed, even in your poverty state. See how you can help and give to other people. Only sow on instruction of the Holy Spirit, because then you know that the ground is fruitful. Do not sow out of obligation, don't be manipulated to sow. Remember you cannot receive from God if your hands are closed towards your fellow brother. Sometimes it hurts to sow, but sow anyway by being led by the Holy Spirit.

To sow in faith is so very important in life; do not fear to sow - God will see you through. Call your seed a name; like I sowed this seed to receive $7000 for the December holidays, or like God said, I sow Jesus to reap many sons. Now you praise and thank God for the harvest with peace in your heart. Having peace will result in a good outcome, far above you might think or pray for.

Luk 6:38 "Give, and will be given to you; good measure, pressed down, shaken together, and running over, will they pour into the bosom. For with the measure you deal out, it will be measured back to you."

Act 20:35 "…., how He Himself said, It is more blessed to give than to receive."

I suggest keep on sowing and trust God for the harvest

Revelation 14
To whom shall we sow?
To the church or the house?

We are all supposed to sow; it's in sowing that we can reap a harvest. You cannot receive from God if your hands are closed for your neighbour. A closed hand cannot receive!!! Have you heard people say: You must sow where you receive the Word of God or you must sow in fruitful ground?

God said that we must give tithes and offerings so that there can be food in His **house. Mal 3:10** „ Bring all the tithes into the **storehouse**, that there may be food in My **house** and prove Me now by it, says the Lord of hosts, if I will not open the windows of heaven for you and pour you out a blessing…"

But God does not need food!!! **Who is this House He is talking about?**

We as individuals are all **Houses** of God, we need food in our **houses,** and we are the **House** of God.

2 Co 5:1… „we have a building of God, a **house** not made with hands, eternal in the heavens."

1 Pe 2:5 „[*Come*] and, like living stones, be yourselves built
[*into*] a spiritual **house**… „

To whom shall we sow?
God is telling us to open our hands, to give to one another so that there will be food in our **houses**. God says we must listen to the instruction of His Holy Spirit to sow to whoever He shows us to. If you sow to an individual or a Church organization so be it. That ground is then fruitful ground, because it is on His instruction.

My personal opinion about tithes and offerings is: Tithes and offerings is Old Testament. In the New Testament, God **gave** His Son, so must we also just **give** as Holy Spirit instructs us.

Revelation 15
Are you focusing on lack or abundance?

I was talking to our Father God and I said: God I don't want to have this financial lack in my life anymore, so I rebuked lack and commanded abundance to come in, in Jesus name. That night I had a dream. I was at a friend's house and in his house he had his own mini supermarket. This supermarket had trays where all the different types of bread were lying, it had fridges where all the different types of soft drinks were, and it had aisles where all the different types of canned foods were stacked. He invited me to go shopping. We took grocery baskets and started shopping. When we were finished, we passed the cash register and did not pay for any of the goods. And God said: "That is abundance".

Isa 55:1 "Wait and listen, everyone who is thirsty! Come to the waters; and he who has no money, come, buy and eat! Yes, come, buy [*priceless, spiritual*] wine and milk without money and without price [*simply for the self-surrender that accepts the blessing*]". [*Rev. 21:6, 7; 22:17.*]

We say: "I only have $20 for petrol for my car". Why don't we say next time: "I am going to fill the tank of my car to the brim". We say: "It's my daughter's birthday; my budget allows me to buy her that cheap no name brand doll". Why don't we say: "This birthday I am going to buy my daughter that beautiful expensive Barbie doll?"

When we go to a restaurant we first look at how much money we have and the prices of the meals [the lack], why don't we say before we go: "I am not a "cheapo", I am going to eat what I want, not what the lack of money in my purse prescribes".

I am not saying go and make debt to do all these abundant things, I am saying let's start trusting God to provide abundance, and thank Him until it manifests. Let's start speaking abundance and not lack in our finances until it manifests.

Then when the money for the petrol, birthday present or meals is supplied by God, do not use it on something else, use it for what it was intended for so that you can see and realize that God is supplying in abundance.

A week later: I needed 2 tyres for my car. I told God I needed 4 tyres for my car, please provide 4 tyres.**[Focusing on abundance]**. With peace in my heart I knew He would provide. Then God told me to go to the tyres dealer and get a quotation, so I did. Two days later I visited a friend's house.

He asked if I needed tyres. I said yes, and he gave me 4 new tyres!!! **God want us to focus on Him, not our lack. Praise God.**

Ps 118:25 "Save now, we beseech You, O Lord; send now prosperity, O Lord, we beseech You, and give to us success!"

Ps 23:1 "A Psalm of David. THE LORD is my Shepherd [*to feed, guide, and shield me*], I shall not lack."

Ps 23:5 "… You anoint my head with oil; my [*brimming*] cup runs over."

Ps23:6 "Surely only goodness, mercy, and unfailing love shall follow me all the days of my life."

Mal 3:10 "…Test me in this and see if I don't open up heaven itself to you and pour out blessings beyond your wildest dreams."

Note: A month before, I bought 2 tyres for a friend of mine.
Sowing seed is very important.

2 Co 9:10 "And [*God*] Who provides seed for the sower and bread for eating will also provide and multiply your [*resources for*] sowing and increase the fruits of your righteousness [*which manifests itself in active goodness, kindness, and charity*]". [*Isa. 55:10; Hos. 10:12.*]

Revelation 16
The fear of running out!!!

We always fear that we are going to come short; we are constantly holding back for we don't know what will happen tomorrow. We constantly fear about our financial state. You can be as poor as a church mouse or a rich millionaire, we fear the tomorrows. Have you seen a poor man stressed out of not having food in his house? Some rich men get stressed out not having enough, quarrelling over a few dollars" discount. That's called the fear of running out!!!

It's sickening; it's a sickness to fear lack. We say we cannot sow this money, because we will run short this month; when we run a 2 mile course we say to ourselves we must not go full out, because we will run out of breath, we go for a drive and can only go 60 mp/h because we must save petrol for another trip tomorrow. We are supposed to trust in God's supply.

God did not make lack; he made things in abundance. Lack and the fear of running out is all in the mind. God made the seed on trees, a man's sperm, the stars in the universe, to proclaim his glory and abundance.

I heard a story about the google.com owners. They had a question when they were in South Africa for the Soccer World Cup. They phoned this guy who could help them, but he could not help them over the phone, so they sent their own plane to fetch him, not thinking twice about the fear of running out of money.

Our trust should be in God – not fear of running out. I am not saying be stupid with your money, I am saying listen to Holy Spirit. When He says sow you sow, when He says buy that car, don't fear you will run out, and buy it!!!

Jesus was at a wedding in Cana and all the wine ran out!!! The people were already drunk, but Jesus made between 100 -160 litres of the best wine. In this He proclaimed His glory and abundance.

That day they did not run out!!!

Joh 2:1 "On the third day there was a wedding at Cana of
Galilee, and the mother of Jesus was there."

Joh 2:3 "And when the wine was all gone, the mother of Jesus said to Him, They have no more wine!"

Joh 2:6 "Now there were six water pots of stone standing there, as the Jewish custom of purification (ceremonial washing) demanded, holding twenty to thirty gallons apiece.
[About 18-27 gallons or 80-120 litres]."

Joh 2:7 "Jesus said to them, fill the water pots with water.
So they filled them up to the brim."

Joh 2:11 "This, the first of His signs (miracles, wonderworks),Jesus performed in Cana of Galilee, and manifested His glory."

Note: My idea about financial freedom and abundance is: earning $10000 or even $1000000 per month is putting a limit on God's abundance and God is unlimited. It is when I go to my father and ask him, that I receive everything I ask. I put my total trust in him to provide in the smallest and the biggest. That is financial freedom, free from making our own plans to provide and trusting God to provide in abundance, not saying you must not work or sow but be led by Holy Spirit.

[Jehovah Jirah = The Lord our Provider and Seer].

Luk 11:10 "For every one that asketh receiveth; and he that seeketh findeth; and to him that knocketh it shall be opened."

Luk 11:11 "If a son shall ask bread of any of you that is a father, will he give him a stone? or if *he ask* a fish, will he for a fish give him a serpent?"

Luk 11:12 "Or if he shall ask an egg, will he offer him a scorpion?"

Luk 11:13 "If ye then, being evil, know how to give good gifts unto your children: how much more shall *your* heavenly Father give the Holy Spirit to them that ask him?"

Revelation 17
Releasing, surrendering your need in prayer, Stop fighting to manifest a favourable outcome

On **19 February,** I asked God for money and a vehicle before **31 March.** I want to visit my friend, Andre Theron, in Namibia, 1800 km away, for his daughter's wedding. I asked God to send someone who will present his vehicle for this trip. **By faith I filled a friend's car with petrol and I sowed $ 260 to my friend Andre, on instruction of the Holy Spirit.**

I released, surrendered the outcome of this prayer in God's hands and praised Him for His goodness.

Testimony 1: On **3 March** another friend of mine, who knew I wanted to go to Namibia, phoned and said one of his friends is moving to Namibia and he wanted me to take his extra car to Namibia, all petrol expenses paid, leaving the car in Namibia.

Outcome: On **30 March** the friend that presented his car cancelled on me, saying he wanted to sell the car here in South Africa.

Testimony 2: One of my friends, Patrick, came to me today, **2 March,** presenting a fantastic, but risky one-time business deal. One of his clients ran into some

cash flow problems and needed $1300 immediately. His client said she would give him $6600 if she can borrow the $1300 from him and as soon as her cheque got cleared, she would pay him the $6600. Patrick
asked me if I would like to go 50/50 and receive a 50% profit share of $3300. So I gave Patrick the $ 650, my share. Patrick told me if this deal went sour, he would give me the $650 back.

Holy Spirit spoke to me and said: "No, Andries, you carry the risk with Patrick, you release, surrender, lose yourself from that $650. If you lose the $ 650, you lose it, but trust Me with no fear in your heart for a favourable outcome".

I told Patrick: „If this deal goes sour, I do not want you to give me back the $650." I released, surrendered that $650 and sowed it as a seed. Not knowing the outcome, but trusting God who said you will reap what you sow.

Outcome: On **30 March** I phoned Patrick and asked about the business deal. He told me he didn't know if and when we would receive the money.

God's outcome of the prayer: Beforehand God sold me on the idea of going with my own car, because the car that was presented was just for one way. Later, on

30 March, money came through for the trip to Namibia. Much more money was released in a totally different way as expected.

God supplied the car and money for the trip. On **3 April** we drove to Namibia. **Praise God.**

Eph 3:20 "Now to Him Who, by the power that is at work within us, is able to do Super-abundantly, far over and above all that we [*dare*] ask or think [*infinitely beyond our highest prayers, desires, thoughts, hopes, or dreams*]."

Testimony 3: A garden rake was stolen out of my garage. I said to God: "Lord I sow, release, and surrender this garden rake". Two weeks later I was driving and next to the road was a big box. I opened the box and there were 5 new garden rakes.

In praying for your need it is very important to release and surrender your need. Stop fighting to manifest a favorable outcome. Reject fear and have peace and trust in God. Your life, your prayer is in His hands. Can He decide what's best for you? Let Him decide the outcome of your prayer and need. His will and outcome is financial abundance, healing and breakthrough if you believe.

Example: When you pray for finances, healing or breakthrough: The **words** you are **praying** and **saying** is a **seed**. When we **fear** and don't **surrender**

the **outcome** and don't **trust** God, we take the **words/prayer/seed** that we **prayed** out of the ground. **This is when we don't receive from God.**

The farmer plants seeds in the ground. He releases, surrenders, loosens himself from that seed.
He releases, surrenders, loosens himself from the outcome and yield of the harvest. The farmer will not take the seeds out of the ground.

Mat 13:9 "…, the evil one comes and snatches away what was sown in his heart. This is what was sown along the roadside."

Luk 8:11 "Now the meaning of the parable is this: The seed is the Word of God."

Example: Abraham received the promise from God: Out of his **seed** he will be called father of nations. He had to **kill/sow/release/surrender** his **seed/Isaac**. He did not give up on that **promise** but, had to **release, surrender** the **outcome** of that **promise in God's hands.** God provided an outcome because Abraham **released and surrendered** his will, need, and seed.

Gen 17:4 "As for me, behold, my covenant *is* with thee, and thou shalt be a father of many nations."

Gen 22:2 "And he said, Take now thy son, thine only Isaac, whom thou lovest, and get thee into the land of

Moriah; and offer him there for a burnt offering upon one of the mountains which I will tell thee of."

Gen 22:13 "And Abraham lifted up his eyes, and looked, and behold behind *him* a ram caught In a thicket by his horns: and Abraham went and took the ram, and offered him up for a burnt offering in the stead of his son."

Gen 22:17 "That in blessing I will bless thee, and in multiplying I will multiply thy seed as the stars of the heaven, and as the sand which *is* upon the sea shore; and thy seed shall possess the gate of his enemies;

Example: Thank God we do not always receive what we dream, ask and pray for: In 1999 we wanted to buy a house, but the bank did not approve the loan. We **released** that house and moved into a two bedroom flat. In 2003/4 we designed, built and moved into our own beautiful house. Today we drove passed that house we could not buy in 1999; we have received so much more in comparison. **Look back for examples in your own life where God did not give you what you dreamed, asked and prayed for, but gave you actually much more.**

Eph 3:20 "Now to Him Who, by the power that is at work within us, is able to do Superabundantly, fa rover and above all that we [*dare*] ask or think [*infinitely beyond our highest prayers, desires, thoughts, hopes, or dreams*]."

Example: You are about to lose your house:
"Father, I ask You to provide me the money to pay
my house by the end of this month. I now surrender
this house and the payment in Your hands. I give this
house to You. I lay it down and stop fighting to keep
the house. I give this house to You before I lose it. I
reject all fear. I will not even worry if I am not going
to stay in this house anymore. My life and house do
not belong to me anymore. With peace and trust in
my heart I know that You will never leave me and
that You will provide an outcome. I know that my
future is bright. I worship You God for Your
goodness".

**Example: You sometimes get a person who prays a
foolish prayer like:** "Lord, let me win the Lotto or
let someone give me $ 1000000 next week." He then
sows a seed for that. The next week he has not
received anything. Now he is hurt and says to himself
that sowing and trusting God does not work. The
mistake he makes is that God will not give him
something that will probably hurt him at that time in
his life. He loves him too much. Will you give your 5
year old child a hunting knife if he asks for it? What
we must do when we pray for money, is we must sow
on instruction of Holy Spirit and **release** that
outcome of what you are praying for into God's
hands. **God's outcome is abundance.**

Luk 11:11 "For what father of you, *if* the son asks
bread, will he give him a stone? Or if *he asks* for a
fish, will he give him a snake for a fish?"

Example: We all have heard stories like: A married couple struggling to have children. Going to doctors and fertilization clinics, but no success. Until they **release the outcome, desire, dream to have a child** and soon after the result is pregnant.

Example: A person is on his sick bed about to die, fighting for his life. As soon as that person **releases/surrenders** his life and says: "Okay God you can take my life, I release my life in Your hands". It is then that his healing starts to manifest.

Mat 16:25 "For whoever is bent on saving his life shall lose it; and whoever loses his life for My sake shall find it."

Joh 21:22 "Jesus said to him, If I want him to stay (survive, live) until I come, what is that to you?"

Joh 21:23 "So word went out among the brethren that this disciple was not going to die; yet Jesus did not say to him that he was not going to die, but, If I want him to stay (survive, live) till I come, what is that to you?"

Example: Jesus is going to be crucified: Jesus prayed: "let this cup pass". He **released, surrendered** the **outcome** of His prayer into Fathers hands. He laid His will and life down with no fighting into Fathers hands and was crucified. **The outcome of His prayer was that God saved humanity.**

Mar 14:36 "And He was saying, Abba, Father, everything is possible for You. Take away this cup from Me; yet not what I will, but what You [*will*]."
My family and I pray like this:

- We first sow a seed **if instructed by Holy Spirit.**
[Remember: A prayer is a seed]

- We put our needs on paper, lay hands on it and stick it on the fridge.

- We put a time limit on it.
- We reject all fear regarding the outcome of the prayer request.

- **Important: We release the outcome over this need in God's hands. His will and outcome is healing, prosperity in His way, if we believe Him. Trying to manifest an outcome will put judgment, condemnation, fear, confusion, discouragement and guilt on you. Release the outcome.** ☐ We praise God expecting His favorable outcome.
- We remind God of His promises with peace in our hearts and confess God's Word out of rest, not out of stress.

Your responsibility: To sow seed in faith not fear, financially or by means of prayer.
Your responsibility: To release that seed and the outcome of that seed and praise God.
God's responsibility: To grow and manifest the outcome of that seed.

Your responsibility: To receive the harvest of that seed.

1 Co 3:6 "I planted, Apollos watered, but God was making it grow and gave the increase."

Revelation 18
You cannot manipulate seed sown- God grows the seed to be harvested

God spoke to me and said: Andries, you cannot manipulate seed sown. You cannot tell the seed how it must grow or how much harvest it must yield or when the harvest must be. You have to release your seed in faith, without any fear or doubt in your heart. You can only water the seed by trusting in God and thanking God for a favorable outcome.

God said to me: The farmer plants seeds in the ground. He releases, surrenders, loosens himself from that seed. He releases, surrenders, loosens himself from the outcome and yield of the harvest. The farmer will not to take the seeds out of the ground.

Joh 12:24 "Truly, truly, I say to you, unless a grain of wheat falls into the ground and dies, it abides alone; but if it dies, it brings forth much fruit."

As soon as you sow the seed, it's not your seed anymore, it's God's seed and only He can make it grow. You just water that seed through thanksgiving and trusting Him and receiving the harvest.

1 Co 3:6 "I planted, Apollos watered, but God was making it grow and [He] gave the increase."

Luk 8:11 "Now the meaning of the parable is this: The seed is the Word of God."

The **word/prayer** of finances, healing or breakthrough you are **praying** for is a **seed**. When we **pray** the **word** of finances, healing or breakthrough over our lives, we need to release or surrender the outcome of that prayer in God's hands, with no fear in our hearts. We know that God will release finance, healing or breakthrough in His way, because **His word says so.**

When we fear and don't trust God, we take the **word/seed** that we **prayed** for, out of the ground and manipulate it. We cut ourselves off from God's promises. **This is when we don't receive from God.** Sometimes a seed sown got stolen by the devil. It's in these situations that you release/surrender that seed in God's hands.

Testimony: A garden rake was stolen out of my garage. I told God that I sow, release, and surrender this garden rake. Two weeks later I was driving and next to the road was a big box. I opened the box and there were five new garden rakes!!

Testimony: I used to work with a lady friend of ours, Lara, in 2007. About every morning we used to pray and agree with her for a Peugeot car. She had the picture of this car in her Bible. Only in 2012 did she receive her car.

Testimony: A house that has been standing for 150 years was broken down, a light rain came, three days later the seed of 150 years germinated and sprung forth. **Seed sown never dies.**

If God tells us to sow a seed, **financially,** or sow a **"word" seed in prayer** for healing or breakthrough. He wants us to **release, surrender** that **financial seed** or that **word/prayer/seed for healing** into His hands and trust Him for the favorable outcome. We must trust and know that our lives are kept in His hand. We must have total peace that our seed will grow and will be harvested in season.

Gal 6:9 "And let us not lose heart and grow weary and faint in acting nobly and doing right, for in due time and at the appointed season we shall reap, if we do not loosen and relax our courage and faint."

Revelation 19
A cry for help!!!
How to get you prayers answered by God

Example: On **14 October 2003** we started building our dream house. Because we thought it would be finished in 3 months, we cut all cost and moved into a double garage. The building process proceeded very slowly. Many difficulties faced us, such as the brick factory running out of bricks, the act of ownership getting lost, the builder finding another job. After **crying** to God to help us finish the home, after fasting, speaking in tongues - nothing happened. One night in that garage, while my family was sleeping, I spoke to God and said: „**Lord, I will stay in this garage with my family until You take me out of here. It's okay.' The result of my decision?** On **14 October 2004** we moved into our house - exactly a year since we started building.

Example: Have you ever seen the program on Satellite TV:"**I should not be alive**"? All the stories are true and based on people who were trapped in dire situations, but rescued eventually. This one story is about two friends climbing the Alpine mountains. They got stuck and could not move for 7 days because of a severe storm. A helicopter came but they were not noticed. On the edge of dying,

they decided to make peace with dying alone on the mountain. The end result: As soon as they decided to make peace, suddenly a helicopter spotted them and they got saved in a nick of time just before dying.

Example: David cried before God to let his son live, but after 7 days he died. **The end result:** Another son was born, Salomon.

2 Sa 12:16 "David therefore be sought God for the child; and

David fasted and went in and lay night on the floor."

2 Sa 12:19 "But when David saw that his servants whispered, he perceived that the child was dead. So he said to them, is the child dead? And they said, He is."

2 Sa 12:20 "Then David arose from the floor, washed, anointed himself, changed his apparel, and went into the house of the Lord and worshiped. Then he came to his own house, and when he asked, they set food before him, and he ate."

2 Sa 12:22 "David said, While the child was still alive, I fasted and wept; for I said, Who knows whether the Lord will be gracious to me and let the child live?"

Example: I needed a breakthrough in ministry and business in my life. I decided I was going to lie before God for 7 days, asking Him, begging, **crying**

before Him for this breakthrough. No breakthrough
came. A week later I decided I would fast for
8 days for this breakthrough. No breakthrough came.
On 2 May 2013 I gave up; I quit; I shut down my cell
phone and PC and did not do anything for that day,
NOTHING happened. On 31 July I said to God:
"Lord I repent, my focus was not on You and
whenever you want to give me a breakthrough I will
be patient and wait". The next day breakthrough
suddenly appeared.

If your prayers don't get answered you feel like
quitting, but God said this to me: „You must quit".
BUT people say differently. They say: **never, ever,
ever quit.** Well, I began to totally disagree with them.
I quit every day when I face a struggle. I am not
saying **stop** what you are doing do your **best
consistently** to get a breakthrough or healing, but
never, ever trust in yourself and your ability to give
you that breakthrough or healing. I am saying:
"Never, ever, ever, ever quit hoping, trusting and
relying that God alone will save, heal, deliver and
give you a breakthrough". I am saying: "Stop
fighting- the only fight there is a fight of faith".

Jer 17:5 "Thus says the Lord: Cursed is the strong
man who trusts in and relies on frail man, making
weak [*human*] flesh his arm, and whose mind and
heart turn aside from the Lord."

Jer 17:7 "Blessed is the man who believes in, trusts in, and relies on the Lord, and whose hope and confidence the Lord is."

After all this I still asked God **what I must do to get my prayers answered. God spoke to me:,,** My people are **crying** for help. The **cry** is nothing less than **fear** and **unbelief**. The currency God works with is **faith** and **trust**, not **crying.** What you need to do is speak **peace** to your struggling, to your mountain; not **crying,** but **trusting God** for a breakthrough and your prayers will be answered at the **appointed time.**

No more crying or begging - speak peace to your fears of the future, your healing, your finances, your breakthrough in Jesus" name. Remember if there is no peace there is no change in your situation.

Heb 11:6 "But without faith it is impossible to please and be satisfactory to Him. For whoever would come near to God must believe that God exists and that He is the rewarder of those who earnestly and diligently seek Him."

Ecc 9:10 "Whatever your hand finds to do, do it with all your might…"

Ecc 9:11 "I returned and saw under the sun that the race is not to the swift nor the battle to the strong neither is bread to the wise nor riches to men of intelligence and understanding nor favour to men of skill; but time and chance happen to them all."

Prayer: Lord I might not understand Your Will; I might not understand the reason why I have not received my healing or breakthrough. I just have to trust Your ways and timing. No more crying, no more fear. My faith is in You Lord, Your Will be done. I speak peace over all my fears in Jesus name. Amen

Revelation 20
The Un-answered Prayer

Mat 26:39 "... My Father, if it is possible, let this cup pass away from Me; nevertheless, not what I will [*Not what I desire*], but as You will and desire."

Mat 26:42 "A second time He went away and prayed, My Father, if this cannot pass by unless I drink it, Your will be done."

Jesus prayed and God did not answer His prayer. Why? God had a bigger purpose. It was to save humanity and to send Holy Spirit.

John 16:7 "I am telling you nothing but the truth when I say it is profitable for you that I go away. Because if I do not go away, the Comforter will not come to you; but if I go away, I will send Him to you."

Jesus' prayer was answered by God through His suffering on the cross.

Do you feel that your prayer is hitting the roof and not reaching
God's ears?
Do you sometimes feel like saying: God, what are You doing?
How must we handle unanswered prayers?

We pray to God to release finances: It does not happen. Why? Perhaps we are stingy and fearful to give. God's bigger purpose is that we should start sowing and giving first and trusting Him for a harvest and this will not happen if He gives us finances before we have learned to sow. We must first start sowing and giving in our state of lack before the financial breakthrough manifests.

Luk 6:38 "Give, and will be given to you; good measure, pressed down, shaken together, and running over, will they pour into the bosom. For with the measure you deal out, it will be measured back to you."

We pray to God to help us lose weight. It does not happen. Why? Perhaps God's bigger purpose is that we should rule first over our eating habits, because He has already given us the
Spirit of self-control. **[2 Tim 1:7]**

We pray to God to heal us. It does not happen. Why? Perhaps
God's bigger purpose is that we must first release this burden, focus on Him and not on the sickness, and just have peace and know that He actually has already healed us and thank Him for this and then the healing will manifest. **[Is: 53]**

Testimony: Cobus, a friend of mine, had a pain in his foot and everyone prayed for him and nothing happened. He still experienced pain. So he told me about this. Holy Spirit told me that we should pray for wisdom, so we did. He came to know that the acid level in his blood was too high, and because of that his foot pained. He changed medication, and the problem was solved. **God obtains His purpose by not always answering or giving what we ask, because there is a bigger purpose.**

But His will and purpose is to prosper, heal, etc. **But** why is it sometimes not happening? I think **Trust, Peace, Wisdom and**
Timing are the keys. The problem is also the way we
think breakthrough and outcome should happen.

We must thank God that our prayers are not answered in the way we want them answered.
Will God give you a stone if you ask bread? Will you give your 5 year old child a big hunting knife to play with?

I have seen in my own life that God never answers or gives breakthroughs or outcomes the way we think it should happen. It always happens in a better way, because He is God and He knows best for us, even if we don't agree at the time.

Eph 3:20 "Now to Him Who, by the power that is at work within us, is able to do superabundantly, far over and above all that we ask or think [*infinitely beyond our highest prayers, desires, thoughts, hopes, or dreams*]."

1 Pe 5:10 "The suffering won't last forever. It won't be long before this generous God who has great plans for us in Christ-eternal and glorious plans they are!--will have you put together and on your feet for good."

Why do we sometimes feel led by God in faith to venture into something and in the end it does not work out?

Heb 11:36 "Others had to suffer the trial of mocking and scourging and even chains and imprisonment."

Heb 11:37 "They were stoned to death; they were lured with tempting offers; they were sawn asunder; they were slaughtered by the sword; they had to go about wrapped in the skins of sheep and goats, utterly destitute, oppressed, cruelly treated."

Heb 11:38 "Of whom the world was not worthy--roaming over the desolate places and the mountains, and in caves and caverns and holes of the earth."

Heb 11:39 "And all of these, though they won divine approval by their faith, **did not receive the fulfilment of what was**
promised."

Heb 11:40 "Because God had us in mind and had something better and greater in view for us, so that they should not come to perfection apart from us."

Our responsibility is to have peace and totally trust in God, knowing He has a bigger, better purpose. **His own way, His own time.**

1 Jo 5:14 "And this is the confidence which we have in Him: that if we ask anything according to His will (in agreement with His own plan), He listens to and hears us."

1 Jo 5:15 "And if we know that He listens to us in whatever we ask, we also know that we have there quests made of Him."

Father, I Andries, one of your sons, prayerfully ask you that everyone that reads this letter will receive breakthrough in finance, healing and restoration in all other areas needed in Jesus name. I pray that your will and your outcome be done in these areas. Father, we now take your loving peace in these situations. We release these outcomes and timings of manifestation in your hands and we thank you now that you love and care for us. We trust You lord with these situations. Thank you that whatever happens, the outcome will be favorable. We praise and thank you Lord. Amen.

Revelation 21
Don't take offence; don't give offence – The ministry of reconciliation

2 Co 5:18 "And all things *are* of God, who hath reconciled us to himself by Jesus Christ, and hath given to us the ministry of reconciliation." ☐ How many were hurt by someone?
* How many were hurt in church?
* How many took offence?
* How many gave offence?

Don't take offence – Reconcile

I asked my friend Hannes, a non-Christian, if I could buy money currency from him at way below market price, actually manipulating him because we are friends. He indirectly told me that it was a slap in his face asking such a thing, I am a son of God and must not make myself cheap or sell myself short in asking discount. I was so humiliated and angry by what he had said. I **took offence.** God spoke to me: My son, Hannes is right, you are not a scavenger, you are one of my blessed sons. So I **reconciled** with Hannes. I asked him forgiveness for putting him on the spot. I thanked God for the correction, and thanked my friend for correcting me.

Act 24:16 "And herein do I exercise myself, to have always a conscience void of offence toward God, and *toward* men." **Rom 14:20** "For meat destroy not the work of God. All things indeed *are* pure; but *it is* evil for that man who eats with offence."

Don't give offence – Reconcile

A pastor's wife was talking badly about me behind my back. She **gave offence** through her actions towards me.
Reconciliation came when I phoned her husband and told him, his wife had a loose mouth, talking behind my back. She phoned me, and when I spoke to her, I did it with authority. I told her to come to my house and apologize. She came, stood on her knees before me saying: „Andries, I ask before God that you will forgive me." I forgave her, did **not take offence**, we prayed together and **reconciliation** happened.

2 Co 6:3 "Giving no offence in anything, that the ministry be not blamed."

1 Co 10:32 "Give none offence, neither to the Jews, nor to the
Gentiles, nor to the church of God."

Mat 18:7 "Woe unto the world because of offences! for it must needs be that offences come; but woe to that man by whom the offence cometh!"

Ministry of Reconciliation

We, our sin, Jesus took and nailed to the cross. He should have **taken offence**, because it was not His sin, but ours that He took on Him. He loved us that much not to **take offence**. He did everything to cleanse, forgive and **reconcile** us to Father God.

2 Co 5:18 "But all things are from God, Who through Jesus
Christ reconciled us to Himself and gave to us the ministry of reconciliation [*that by word and deed we might aim to bring others into harmony with Him*]."

2 Co 5:19 "It was God in Christ, reconciling and restoring the world to favor with Himself, not counting up and holding against [*men*] their trespasses [*but cancelling them*], and committing to us the message of reconciliation (of the restoration to favor)."

Having offence – No Reconciliation

You can only **have offence** against the devil; he is the enemy, not people.

Mat 16:23 "But he turned, and said unto Peter, Get thee behind me, Satan: thou art an offence unto me: for thou savourest not the things that be of God, but those that be of men."

The devil wants to break up the Body of Christ. This mostly results from misunderstandings disguised by the devil to break up the body of Jesus Christ. We as

Christians must not allow that. You cannot cut a person off; he is part of the Body of Christ. We as Christians must exercise reconciliation.

Eph 6:12 "For we are not wrestling with flesh and blood, but against the despotisms, against The powers, against the world rulers of this present darkness, against the spirit forces of wickedness in the heavenly sphere."
You will always find two sides of understanding and misunderstanding. You will find that these misunderstandings can be dissolved if everyone states his case and **practice love, forgiveness and reconciliation and gets a common ground of understanding.**

Pro 18:17 "He who states his case first seems right, until his rival comes and cross-examines him."

Ask ourselves this when you feel offended or hurt: WWJD - What Would Jesus Do?

1 Pe 4:8 "Above all things have intense and unfailing love for one another, for love covers a multitude of sins [*forgives and disregards the offenses of others*]."

Mat 6:14 "For if you forgive people their trespasses, your heavenly Father will also forgive you."

Mat 6:15 "But if you do not forgive others their trespasses, neither will your Father forgive you your trespasses."

Revelation 22
„In confrontation & differences, wait until I give you the words to speak", says God

I was in grade 10 in school. This one boy Gary Webb and I used to fight often. I was always ready for a confrontation with him. Every time I was outsmarted by him and got beaten up badly, my eyes got beaten shut. This did not help my ego and self-esteem and I started hating him, but eventually I forgave him and gave my life to Jesus.

Many years later God asked me: "Andries, do you know what you can learn out of that situation of confrontation and differences where you got beaten up by Gary Webb? ".

I said:" Speak to me Lord". God said: "Don't always be ready for confrontation or a fight and speak out and say your own say, but wait for My Holy Spirit to speak through you, if you speak out of your own heart your eyes will be beaten shut".

God said there is going to be confrontation and difference between people because He made people individuals with different ideas and it is all right, but it is the way that these differences will be solved that will make the difference. Especially churches, this one preaches rapture that one teaches everlasting life and then we build walls between fellow Christian brothers.

Then we say: „This is our kingdom and that is your kingdom, we don't mix with each other because we differ in interpreting the scriptures. So we are building our own kingdoms because we say we are right and that preacher is wrong. Is it not God's kingdom? Who says you don't miss it on some points? Paul taught the Corinthians differently than he taught the Ephesians because of their level of understanding.

Does the Bible not say in **1 Co 13:12** "...Now I know in part (imperfectly), but then I shall know and understand fully and clearly, even in the same manner as I have been fully and clearly known and understood [by God]."

If you differ with someone don't build walls, but forgive. We are not supposed to operate apart from each other. We are the body of Jesus Christ, one in Christ and need to love and care for each other even if we preach differently.

Joh 17:21 "That they all may be one, [just] as You, Father, are in Me and I in You, that they Also may be one in Us, so that the world may believe and be convinced that You have sent Me."

Joh 17:22 "I have given to them the glory and honor which You have given Me, that they may be one [even] as We are one."

God says: "If you differ and have confrontation with someone, don't speak your mind or build walls and your own kingdom; wait for My Holy Spirit to give you the words to say and those words will make a massive impact in that person's life and your eyes will not be beaten shut, because you speak not out of yourself but out of My Holy Spirit".
Mar 13:11 "Now when they take you [to court] and put you under arrest, do not be anxious beforehand about what you are to say nor [even] meditate about it; but say whatever is given you in that hour and at the moment, for it is not you who will be speaking, but the Holy Spirit."

Revelation 23
Get a common ground of understanding in marriage and relationships

My wife Ronel and I had a huge fight yesterday about an insignificant issue. When friends visit us I think it's just good manners to help her wash the dishes after dinner, but she disagrees. She wants to serve them and feels they do not have to do anything after dinner, as she would clean up all by herself.

Then after a heated argument, we came to the root of the real issue. **I think she does not want to admit when she is wrong and she thinks I want to manipulate and overpower her decisions.** The devil enjoys bringing in misunderstanding like this. I think this way, she thinks that way. Remember there are always two sides of a coin.

Pro 18:17 "He who states his case first seems right, until his rival comes and cross-examines him."

So the issue was left unresolved. I went my way and she her way. Holy Spirit started speaking to me. He said if I wanted to resolve this issue, I shouldn't try to change her outlook on this, but get to a place of **common understanding. In any relationship if you want change you change first. Ask your partner, yourself and Holy Spirit in which area you need to**

change to better the relationship. If that change means rebuke or submission, do it.
I went to her and told her to sit down so that we could find a **common ground of understanding**. I would not change her outlook and she would not change mine. We would find a **common ground** where we both would be happy with the outcome.

Long story short, we decided when friends visited, they would help packing up the dishes, but not wash them. What Holy Spirit taught me is not to change a person, because it is only Holy Spirit who can change someone. You must just find a **common ground**.

Joh 16:8 "And when that One comes, He will convict the world concerning sin, and concerning righteousness, and concerning judgment."

Today my friend Dave came to visit and I shared how Holy Spirit resolved this issue. He said the way I did it, was absolutely biblical. He said when God said I would meet you at the mercy seat, God did not say He would manipulate or overpower you. God said we should talk about this issue, because we are in a loving relationship. Let's find a **common ground of understanding**.

Exo 25:21 "You shall put the mercy seat on the top of the ark, and in the ark you shall put the testimony that I will give you."

Exo 25:22 "There I will meet with you and, from above the mercy seat, from between the two cherubim that are upon the ark of the Testimony, I will speak intimately with you of all which I will give you in commandment to the Israelites."

Isa 1:18 "Come now, and let us reason together, says the Lord. Though your sins are like scarlet, they shall be as white as snow; though they are red like crimson, they shall be like wool."

And the common ground is His grace and His mercy!!!!!!!!!!!!!!!!!!!!!!!

Revelation 24
Who or what is the church / house of God?

Listen, hear me out!!!
You must **go to church, the house of God.**
Let's **have church**.
You must **belong to a church.**

If we are the Body of Jesus Christ, if we are **the church, the house of God.**

How can we as **the church go to ourselves?**
How can you as **the church have yourself?**
How can you as **the church belong to yourself**? We belong to God.

Going to church is visiting friends, family, and strangers and talking, praying and sharing about God.

Having Church or fellowship is making an impact in someone's life, praying, giving and sharing with someone.

Belonging to a church is being one in faith with fellow believers, the Body of Christ.

Joh 17:21 "That they all may be one, as You, Father, are in Me and I in You, that they also may be one in

Us, so that the world may believe and be convinced that You have sent Me."

Joh 17:22 "I have given to them the glory and honor which
You have given Me, that they may be one as We are one?"
Joh 17:23 "I in them and You in Me, in order that they may become one and perfectly united, that the world may know and recognize that You sent Me and that You have loved them as You have loved Me."

Too much emphasis is placed on **going to church, having church and belonging to a church.** We as the church must make an impact and difference where we are. You are the representative of Christ on the earth. Start **being the church** where you are.

2 Co 5:1 "For we know that if the tent which is our earthly home is destroyed, we have from God a building, a house not made with hands, eternal in the heavens."

Heb 9:24 "For Christ has not entered into a sanctuary made with hands, only a copy and pattern and type of the true one, but into heaven itself, now to appear in the presence of God on our behalf."

On Sundays you sit in a **church building** year after year receiving and giving nothing out. The living word you receive will rot inside you if you don't start giving out.

I am not saying do not go to a **church building /organization**. I am saying stop being a bench warmer and start making an impact in people's lives. Jesus went **out and did** miracles. When you start **doing** something for someone else, or giving of yourself to someone where you are, it takes the focus off your own problem and before you knows it, your problem is sorted.

Act 1:1 "The former treatise have I made, O Theophilus, of all that Jesus began both to **do and teach.**"
I see it like this: In the time of the building of the Tower of Babel, God came and changed their languages, God saw it as **positive**, and the people saw it as **negative**. God wanted to fill the earth. The people wanted to stay in **one building**. God wants us not to just receive; He wants us to go out and **do** miracles in His name, 7 days a week, making an impact where we are.

The church must operate like network marketing. Jesus duplicated Himself in 12 disciples, the 12 duplicated themselves in 3000 and so on, each **being the church** on its own and making an impact where he is at. This is a much better way to spread the Gospel through duplication.

Mar 16:15 "And He said to them, Go into all the world and preach and publish openly the good news (the Gospel) to every creature."

Mar 16:16 "He who believes and is baptized will be saved; but he who does not believe will be condemned."

Mar 16:17 "And these attesting signs will accompany those who believe: in My name they will drive out demons; they will speak in new languages."

Mar 16:18 "They will pick up serpents; and if they drink anything deadly, it will not hurt them; they will lay their hands on the sick, and they will get well."

Revelation 25
You are the church - make an impact!!!
Being manipulated paying tithes, giving offerings or first fruits wasting your seed

God spoke to me saying: "Jesus My Son did not give a mere tithe or an offering, He gave His life. **God said:** You are free from giving tithes and offerings, but not free to give, only give by the leading of Holy Spirit".

Mat 17:24 "When they arrived in Capernaum, the collectors of the half shekel [*the temple tax*] went up to Peter and said, Does not your Teacher pay the half shekel?"

Mat 17:25 "He answered, yes. And when he came home, Jesus spoke to him first, saying, What do you think, Simon? From whom do earthly rulers collect duties or tribute--from their own sons or from others not of their own family?"

Mat 17:26 "And when Peter said, from other people not of their own family, Jesus said to him, then the sons are exempt".

Mat 17:27 "However, in order not to give offense and cause them to stumble go down to the sea and throw in a hook. Take the first fish that comes up, and when you open its mouth you will find there a shekel. Take it and give it to them to pay the temple tax for Me and for yourself."

Yesterday morning I asked God: "Lord I want to stock my fridge with meat again". Holy Spirit immediately spoke to me:

"Give **ZAR 500** to you friend Uncle Chris". I agreed and asked Holy Spirit just to give me a day or so, I would then sow the money to him. At **10 o'clock** I received a text massage from the bank, **Deposited: ZAR 500.**

That **afternoon** I went to my friend Uncle Chris and sowed the **ZAR 500** into his life.

That **weekend** I ordered the meat, paid with my credit card and stocked my fridge.

The next week I received **$ 500** from my dear sister in Christ, Debbie in the USA.

Thank you my beautiful God!! I worship and praise Your awesome name.

2 Co 9:10 "And [*God*] Who provides seed for the sower and bread for eating will also provide and multiply your [*resources for*] sowing and increase the fruits of your righteousness [*which manifests itself in active goodness, kindness, and charity*]."

If I, **Andries,** or any church or pastor would say to you the following below: you are wasting your seed.

• **You must tithe or give offerings**, because this ministry or my church is fruitful ground.

• **You must tithe and give offerings** so that there can be food in **God's house**. [**Mal 3:10**].

But God does not need food!!! **Who is this House He is talking about?** We as
individuals are all **Houses of God**, we need food in our **houses,** and we are the **House of God**.

2 Co 5:1… „We have a building of God, **a house** not made with hands, eternal in the heavens."

1 Pe 2:5 „[*Come*] and, like living stones, be yourselves built a spiritual **house**…"

☐ **You must give you tithes and offerings** where you receive the **Word of God.** God does not only speak in a church or through a Pastor. He speaks through every person, He speaks through His creation. I often get an awesome **Word** or **Phrase** from Holy Spirit through secular movies.

You are wasting you seed if you sow based on hints by people, manipulations or pity.
Don't be manipulated, only give by the leading of Holy

Spirit. If Holy Spirit tells you to give to your friend, to a beggar or give to your local church, is that fruitful ground? Definitely yes!!!

2 Co 9:7 "Let each one give as he has made up his own mind and purposed in his heart, not reluctantly or sorrowfully or under compulsion, for God loves a cheerful (joyous, ``prompt to do it") giver [*whose heart is in his giving*]."

Must we give? It is critical for your own good to give by the leading of Holy Spirit.

- God sowed his Son and it hurt Him to do it, but He did it and now He reaps many sons.

Sometimes it hurts to sow, but sow anyway.

- You cannot receive from God if your hands are closed to your neighbour **[the church, house of God]**.
- Listen, start sowing now in your state of poverty. See how you can give and help other people **[the church, house of God].**
- If instructed by Holy Spirit to use the seed myself? You can, you are free in Christ.
- Please only sow on the instruction of Holy Spirit, because then that ground you sow into, is fruitful.
- Don't sow out of obligation or manipulation.

Luk 6:38 "Give, and [gifts] will be given to you; good measure, pressed down, shaken together, and running over, will they pour into the bosom. For with the measure you deal out, it will be measured back to you."

If you disagree with me, its okay, I am not here to convince you!!! I only speak out of personal experiences.

Revelation 26
Man of God vs. son of God

Have you heard people say? "That is truly an anointed man of God" **or** "I am a man of God, you must listen to me"
I want to say to you that, that is bull…. It is Old Testament, **or** sometimes it's not the men of God but insecure people exulting these "men of God" above God.

Don't ever be manipulated by these men of God, rather build a relationship with Holy Spirit and step up and be a manifested son of God.

There is a misconception about this. We put pastors, preachers and prophets on pedestals, they are a bit higher than we are, and they are these big men of God. We are looking for anointed men of God that will pray, so we can receive, we are running after these men of God to receive. We are looking in the wrong place for the manifestation of anointing, power and breakthrough; we must look into a deeper intimate relationship with Holy Spirit.
I agree that some pastors have more knowledge about God than ordinary people, but we are actually all sons and daughters of God. No one bigger or better than the other.

No "man of God" is bigger than a "son of God"

We as individuals must grow into a relationship with God and start relying on Holy Spirit to teach us. I am not saying not to listen to your pastor, preacher or prophet, because God is speaking through any one. **I am saying build a relationship with Holy Spirit to receive anointing.**

1 Co 3:5 "What then is Apollos? What is Paul? Ministering servants through whom you believed, even as the Lord appointed to each his task."

1 Co 3:6 "I planted, Apollos watered, but God was making it grow and [*He*] gave the increase."

1 Co 3:7 "So neither he who plants is anything nor he who waters, but God Who makes it grow and become greater."

1 Co 3:8 "He who plants and he who waters are equal, yet each shall receive his own reward, according to his own labor."

1 Co 3:9 "For we are fellow workmen with and for God; you are God's garden and vineyard and field under cultivation, God's building."

We should not run to a man of God for healing or breakthrough, we must run to God, we must grow in a relationship with Holy Spirit. God is a jealous God and will not share His praises with any man of God. God alone should receive praises.

Jer 17:5 Thus says the Lord: Cursed is the strong man who trusts in and relies on frail man, making weak flesh his arm, and whose mind and heart turn aside from the Lord.

Jer 17:7 "Blessed is the man who believes in, trusts in, and relies on the Lord, and whose hope and confidence the Lord is."
Exo 34:14 "For thou shalt worship no other god: for the
LORD, whose name is Jealous, is a jealous God."

God said His glory will fill the earth – I think there will come a day that God's glory will be so tangible and thick on the earth that people will not run to one place or a specific man of God, but he will go to his next door neighbour and he will ask for prayer and breakthrough will be there and only God will get the praise. I think there will come a day that the glory on earth will be so big, a man will raise someone from the dead and no one will even know that man's name, but they will praise God for the raising; only God will get the praise.

This **power and anointing of God** will manifest in His Body, the church, us, in all sons of God. The glory of God will be seen in all people and God alone will get the praise. God's power and anointing will manifest in you when you grow in your relationship with God. Start making a difference just where you are, let this anointing power flow through you to touch the heart of your neighbour with the love of Jesus Christ.

Give God all the glory, sons of God.

Finally, this glory, this anointing, this power is not available for **men of God** but it's available for all **sons of God**, to all of those who are led by Holy Spirit.

Isa 6:3 "And one cried to another and said, Holy, holy, holy is the Lord of hosts; the whole earth is full of His glory!"

Num 14:21 "But truly as I live and as all the earth shall be filled with the glory of the Lord."

Rom 8:14 "For all who are led by the Spirit of God are sons of God."

Revelation 27
Free from sin and curses

Have you accepted Jesus Christ as your personal Saviour and asked Him to forgive you your sins? Now receive His forgiveness and accept His blood shed for you. After confessing this, you never ask forgiveness for the same sin over and over again. We are not going to put Jesus back on the cross; He has already died for your sins, He is not going to do it again.

God sees you through the blood of Jesus Christ, righteous and perfect. The cross and blood was enough to wash the entire world's sin away.

Stop judging yourself and accept the freedom. Don't be deceived by the devil, you are free. You are free in Jesus Christ.

Ps 103:10 "He has not dealt with us after our sins nor rewarded us according to our iniquities."

Ps 103:11 "For as the heavens are high above the earth, so great are His mercies and loving kindness toward those who reverently and worshipfully fear Him."

Ps 103:12 "As far as the east is from the west, so far has He removed our transgressions from us."

Isa 1:18 "Come now, and let us reason together, says the Lord. Though your sins are like scarlet, they shall be as white as snow; though they are red like crimson, they shall be like wool."

In the Old Testament, bulls" and goats" blood was shed for the remission of the sins of the Israelites. Jesus fulfilled the law. Jesus was not guilty of killing, stealing, lust, gluttony, swearing, addictions to drugs, unforgiveness or any sin you can think of. On the cross He took all these sins of humanity on Him, so we can be free. He died and rose to present His blood to God the Father for the remission of our sins.

Rom 8:2 "For the law of the Spirit of life in Christ Jesus has freed me from the law of sin and death."

Rom 4:15 "For the Law results in wrath, but where there is no law there is no transgression."

Does this freedom of sin and law mean we cannot do what we want? No!!!!! If we keep on sinning, the Law of sowing and reaping applies. For instance, if you keep on stealing, you will eventually get caught and go to jail or if we keep on sleeping around, you will probably get HIV. So if you accepted Jesus in your life and asked forgiveness and you still keep on sinning, you will reap the bad that comes with it on this earth, **but you will not miss Heaven and go to hell because of it**.

Gal 6:7 "Do not be deceived and deluded and misled; God will not allow Himself to be sneered at for whatever a man sows, that and that only is what he will reap."

Gal 6:8 "For he who sows to his own flesh (lower nature, sensuality) will from the flesh reap decay and ruin and destruction, but he who sows to the Spirit will from the Spirit reap eternal life."

God gives us good advice so we can be free from bad choices. Be led by Holy Spirit.

Gal 5:16…But "I say, walk and live in the [Holy] Spirit [responsive to and controlled and guided by the Spirit]; then you will certainly not gratify the cravings and desires of the flesh (of human nature without God)."

Gal 5:17 "For the desires of the flesh are opposed to the [Holy] Spirit, and the Spirit are opposed to the flesh; for these are antagonistic to each other, so that you are not free but are prevented from doing what you desire to do."

Gal 5:18 "But if you are guided (led) by the [Holy] Spirit, you are not subject to the Law."

The choice is yours to live in Christ. Choose right!!!

Deu 30:19 "I call heaven and earth to witness this day against you that I have set before your life and death,

the blessings and the curses; therefore choose life that
you and your descendants may live."

Revelation 28
Must I clean my house of wooden carvings?

Yesterday one of my dearest friends, Gerhard, came to visit me. In our house there are a few wooden, carved cats and also charms dangling in the wind outside. My friend told me to take these cats and charms and burn them, because God says you must not have wooden carvings and idols in your house and the charms outside call bad spirits to you house. So not to offend him I kept quiet. When he left, I prayed to Father and asked:
„Lord, how can I help my friend to be free from this doctrine and law?

The next morning I was lying in bed thinking about this again. Holy Spirit gently explained it to me and told me how to clear this misconception. Holy Spirit told me that we can make idols, gods, wooden carvings of everything in life to worship .

Jesus said you cannot serve God and mammon, but there is nothing wrong with having money, but it's the love of money, keeping it all to yourself, not sowing, being stingy. This makes money an idol or a god you worship.

Luk 16:13 "No servant is able to serve two masters; for either he will hate the one and love the other, or he will stand by and be devoted to the one and despise the other. You cannot serve **God and mammon**."

1 Ti 6:10 "For the **love of money** is a root of all evils; it is through this craving that some have been led astray and have wandered from the faith and pierced themselves through with many acute [mental] pangs."

Say for instance you have a beautiful house and you made that house perfect and when people come to visit, they must be so cautious and clean their feet not to dirty the house, they are barely allowed to move. Then you make an idol or god of that house and that house becomes a stone carving and you worship its beauty.

Say for instance you love sport, but that sport takes up all your family time or precious time with God. Then the sport becomes an idol or a god you worship.

This is exactly the same with **generational or blood line curses**. You are so afraid that your **forefather's worshipped idols** and that evil spirits come on you because of their sins. **Why must we pay for the sins of our forefathers? It is not making sense.**

1   Ch 25:4 "But he did not kill their sons, but as *it is* written in the Law in the book of Moses, where Jehovah commanded, saying, the father shall not die for the sons, nor shall the sons die for *the* fathers, but every man shall die for his own sin."

You take so much time to clean your personal house [your body, soul, spirit] that you forget that Jesus had already set you free when He died on the cross. He has called us to be free and not bound. Stop studying the devil and how to be free from forefather spirits.

Rev 2:24"…Who does not hold this teaching, who have not explored and known the depths of Satan, as they say--I tell you that I do not lay upon you any other burden."

In Jesus" ancestral blood line was a lot of wicked people **[Matt 1: 1-17]**. David was a murderer and an adulterer. Solomon worshiped other gods. **But** Jesus was under no generational blood line or forefather spirit curse. He commanded devils to go, He ruled over Satan. The day when you gave your life to Jesus Christ, He set you free from sin and death. It's your responsibility to choose to believe it or not and to rule in His name. We have His authority.

Deut 30:19 "I call heaven and earth to witness this day against you that I have set before you, life and death, the blessings and the curses; therefore choose life that you and your descendants may live."

Luk 10:19 "Behold! I have given you authority and power to trample upon serpents and scorpions, and over all the power that the enemy; and nothing shall in any way harm you." So when Holy Spirit tells you of something that has a **bondage or hold on you, get rid of it**, but if the wooden cats in your house or the charms have no meaning but being decorative, leave it. Enjoy the beautiful house given to you to testify about it and glorify God. Enjoy your sport with your family, just be free. **Jesus came to set us free, start living free. Please do not make a law or see a devil in everything.**

1 Jo 5:21 "Little children, keep yourselves from idols (false gods)--[from anything and everything that would occupy the place in your heart due to God, from any sort of substitute for Him that would take first place in your life]. Amen (so let it be)."
1 Co 8:4 "In this matter, then, of eating food offered to idols, we know that an idol is nothing (has no real existence) and that there is no God but one."

1 Co 8:5 "For although there may be so-called gods, whether in heaven or on earth, as indeed there are many of them, both of gods and of lords and masters."

1 Co 8:6 "Yet for us there is one God, the Father, Who is the Source of all things and for Whom we have life, and one Lord, Jesus Christ, through and by Whom are all things and
through and by Whom we exist."

Hab 2:18 "What profit is the graven image when its maker has formed it? It is only a molten image and a teacher of lies. For the maker trusts in his own creations [as his gods] when he makes dumb idols."

Hab 2:19 "Woe to him who says to the wooden image, Awake! and to the dumb stone, Arise, teach! Behold, it is laid over with gold and silver and there is no breath at all inside it!"

Revelation 29
Being Led by Holy Spirit?
Making important decisions!!!

A friend of mine, Jaco, told me one morning about one of his friends, a true Christian, who never does anything unless he hears from Holy Spirit. He will sit in his room all day and pray, and if someone visits him and tells him to take a drive or go buy a Coca Cola at the supermarket. He would pray, hear from God and he would then either go or stay put as God instructed him.

God told me that was not the best way being led by Holy Spirit. **If you want to be led by the Holy Spirit, you must decide, take action and behind you, you will hear His voice saying left or right.**

Isa 30:21 "And your ears will hear a word behind you, saying, this is the way; walk in it, when you turn to the right hand and when you turn to the left."

Even Jonah in his disobedience was led by Holy Spirit the right way. Jonah did not listen to God; He did not want to go to Nineveh and decided to go to Tarshish, so the fish swallowed him. He repented; the fish spat him out and only then did he go to Nineveh. Jonah made a decision and in his disobedience God was still behind him to protect and help him.

Jon 1:3 "But Jonah rose up to flee to Tarshish from being in the presence of the Lord."

Jon 1:4 "But the Lord sent out a great wind upon the sea."

Jon 1:15 "So they took up Jonah and cast him into the sea, and the sea ceased from its raging."

Jon 1:17 "Now the Lord had prepared and appointed a great fish to swallow up Jonah. And Jonah was in the belly of the fish three days and three nights."

Jon 2:10 "And the Lord spoke to the fish, and it vomited out
Jonah upon the dry land."

Jon 3:3 "So Jonah arose and went to Nineveh according to the word of the Lord."

Now a slight deviation in one's approach: **If you have prayed and asked God for direction and guidance** in taking that job or moving to another state, and there is **no answer from God to your prayer. You make a decision**, by accepting that job or not, or by moving to another state or not. In this **decision** you trust God to protect you against the **wrong decisions**.

I think in most cases, God is actually waiting for us to **decide** and trust Him to guide our paths. This **decision scenario** is like a mature child making a **decision**. Not like a baby who is too afraid to make any **decisions.**

2 Sa 24:12 "Go and say to David, Thus says the Lord, I hold over you three choices; select one of them, so I may bring it upon you."
Deu 30:19 "I call heaven and earth to witness this day against you that I have set before you, life and death, the blessings and the curses; therefore choose that you and your descendants may live."

Trust God for open or closed doors!!!

Revelation 30
The Spirit of Self-control & Discipline Making a decision!!!

2 Ti 1:7 "For God did not give us a spirit of timidity (of cowardice, of craven and cringing and fawning fear), but of power and of love and of calm and well-balanced mind and discipline and self-control."

At my heaviest I weighed 160 kg. By faith in God, my weight dropped gradually over the years, but I stuck at around 105 kg. I wanted to still lose around 20 kg, but struggled due to bad eating habits. Most of the time I over- ate. My weight went up and down all the time. I did not even want to go away on holidays or weekends, because of the fear of picking up that weight I lost during the week. I lived with that fear every time I stepped on the scale; I wanted to be **free** : free to eat what I want in a controlled manner and not pick up weight. I used all sorts of diets, pills, fasting, gym, running. Nothing worked on the long term.

1 Tim 4:8 "For physical training is of some value, but godliness is useful and of value in everything and in every way, for it holds promise for the present life and also for the life which is to come."

1 Co 6:12-13 "Everything is permissible for me; but not all things are helpful. Everything is lawful for me, but I will not become the slave of anything or be brought under its power. Food for the stomach and the stomach for food, but God will finally end both and bring them to nothing. The body is not intended for sexual immorality, but for the Lord, and the Lord for the body."

On 28 June 2012, I was lying in the bathtub and asked God to show me how to lose this extra weight. God spoke to me: "You do not use My Spirit of self-control and discipline I gave you. It's your responsibility to utilize the Spirit of self-control." "How Lord? How do I use your self-controlling Spirit, God?" God said: "I gave you self-control and discipline. It's your **decision** to use it or not."

I **decided** I would not weigh myself during these 94 days. I **decided** I would use this to establish and utilize a spirit of self-control and discipline God gave me.

By not weighing myself for 94 days, I **learnt** to make a small quality **decision** and stick to it. God did not **teach** me self-control and discipline - He **taught** me to **make a decision and stick to it.**

Steps to take:

- Make a quality decision; write it down because you will forget. In making decisions I test myself on what Holy Spirit taught me in the gym. If you decide to do 15 reps you will do it, if you decide beforehand you will do 10 reps bicep training, you will do just 10. I decided one morning I would just drink protein powders for that day and I wrote it down, so by the end of the day that is exactly what I did.

- Focus on the goal you want to reach and not on how you feel.
- Start small and get small victories, then eventually tackle the big challenges. I decided I would not smoke tomorrow. See your victory, increase the challenge. Get victories and move to bigger ones.
- Stay away from temptation.
- Don't try to stop the bad habit; replace it with a good habit.

Replace bad food with good food. **It takes 21 days to stop a bad habit and learn a good habit.**

- Decide what to do; don't decide what not to do. I decide to eat healthy food today; I decide not to eat any bad foods.
- Don't judge yourself if you fail, you have not totally failed; You have just found another way not to do it. You just try again the next day with smaller goals until you are victorious.
- When you fail there is the grace of God that catches you. If you fail in your approach, failure is a victory in disguise.

Change; learn from that failure and take a revised approach. ☐ Pray for strength.

- Thank God all the time for your victory even when you have failed.

How do you stick to your decisions?

Most important of all: You can say no to temptation, addictions, etc., because of Jesus that strengthens you and knows all temptations you are going through. He says: You can do all things because I strengthen you. So you can say no to temptations and addictions.
Phi 4:13 "I can do all things through Christ which strengthened me."

Heb 4:15 "For we do not have a High Priest Who is unable to understand and sympathize and have a shared feeling with our weaknesses and infirmities and liability to the assaults of temptation, but One Who has been tempted in every respect as we are, yet without sinning."

Jam 1:14 "But every person is tempted when he is drawn away, enticed and baited by his own evil desire (lust, passions)."

Jam 4:7 "So be subject to God. Resist the devil [stand firm against him], and he will flee from you."

Act 24:16 "Therefore I always exercise and discipline myself to have a clear conscience, void of offense toward God and toward men."

Rom 8:5 "For those who are according to the flesh and are controlled by its unholy desires set their minds on and pursue those things which gratify the flesh, but those who are according to the Spirit and are controlled by the desires of the Spirit set their minds on and seek those things which gratify the Holy Spirit."

My testimony: I wanted to stop smoking. Every day I wrote on a paper: "I have stopped smoking, I will never smoke again." I stuck it to my wall so I could see it with the date. The next day had barely arrived; I had only stopped for 2 hours, and then I would buy myself cigarettes again. I did this over and over again, failing again and again. Until one day I made a promise to God **[quality decision]** to never smoke again - that day was 8 September 1993 – and I've never smoked again!!

Do you want to stay the same?
Do you want to be addicted to eating, smoking, drinking or drugs?
Make a decision and take that first step to change. God can take the second step with you.

Deut 30:19 "I call heaven and earth to witness this day against you that I have set before you, life and death, the blessings and the curses; therefore choose life that you and your descendants may live."

Holy Spirit, we thank You for total freedom and Self-control in Christ.

A teacher said he was "too stupid to learn anything." He was fired from his first two jobs for being "non-productive." As an inventor, he made 1,000 unsuccessful attempts at inventing the light bulb. When a reporter asked, "How did it feel to fail 1,000 times?" He replied, "I didn't fail 1,000 times. The light bulb was an invention with 1,000 steps."

"Our greatest weakness lies in giving up. The most certain way to succeed is always to try just one more time. "Thomas Edison

Revelation 31
Why Lord why? Why did you let this happen?

On 16 April 2012, I started at a big company with a wonderful challenging job, a great salary and wonderful prospects for the future as a Branch Manager.

This big company was managed by a college friend of mine; he always said in college I would work for him, and I just laughed at this. An hour after the interview they said I had the job. I did not even start at the bottom of the company, but was appointed as Branch Manager. I just thanked God for this wonderful job. Another friend even prophesied before that I will start in a big company. So I just knew this job came from God.

So on 16 April I started, getting training from the outgoing manager. In the first week I saw a lot of unfairness in the company. For example, the maintenance guy has been called out for the past seven years, paying out of his own pocket for petrol, too afraid to say anything. The company is responsible for call out petrol expenses, not him.

I started addressing things like these and told my direct boss that they are not looking after the workers, but only care about the money. I told my boss that if their focus was money, they would lose money, but if their focus was people, money would automatically follow.

These statements and the fact that I directly challenged Top Management made them furious. So they gave me a final warning of Gross Subordination.

That night God spoke to me and told me that I had a problem with authority. The next day I humbly asked them to forgive my outburst and I assured them that I would submit under their authority.

For 23 working days they made my life hell and fear surrounded me, but through faith I rejected all these fears and did my job to the best of my ability. When I did just one little thing wrong they nailed me. I came to the conclusion that their ego was hurt by what I had said. Their intentions became clear - they wanted me out, because my morals and values were different from theirs, and I was not prepared to compromise.

The last morning I drove to work crying. I asked: „Why Lord why?" You gave me this job – did I mess it up? What was wrong with me? Why could I not just shut up if I see people being treated unfairly? Why am I such a failure? I wanted so much to touch the corporate environment and now this happened. I stood up for You Lord and for righteousness. Why Lord? Why did I even start this job? This was supposed to help my family with a better life. WHY LORD WHY?

God spoke so gently to me: „My purpose with this
was successful, you have succeeded."

Rom 11:33 "Oh, the depth of the riches and wisdom
and knowledge of God! How Unfathomable
(inscrutable, unsearchable) are His judgments (His
decisions)! And how untraceable (mysterious,
undiscoverable) are His ways (His methods, His
paths)."
Rom 11:34 "For who has known the mind of the
Lord and who has understood His thoughts, or who
has been His counselor?" God said to me: "I will
leave 99 sheep in the midst of wolves to save one. I
will leave one sheep, You, Andries, in the midst of
wolves, this company, to save that whole company -
your bosses and your friend, because I love them. Did
you succeed? Yes, my son, you did. Your reward will
be big".

Luk 15: "What man of you, if he has a hundred sheep
and should lose one of them, does not leave the
ninety-nine in the wilderness and go after the one that
is lost until he finds it?"

Luk 15:7 "Thus, I tell you, there will be more joy in
heaven over one wicked person who Repents
(changes his mind, abhorring his errors and misdeeds,
and determines to enter upon a better course of life)
than over ninety-nine righteous persons who have no
need of repentance."

Mat 10:16 "Behold, I am sending you out like sheep in the midst of wolves; be wary and wise As serpents, and be innocent as doves."

Mat 10:17 "Be on guard against men; for they will deliver you up to councils and flog you in their synagogues."

Mat 10:19 "But when they deliver you up, do not be anxious about how or what you are to speak; for what you are to say will be given you in that very hour and moment."

Mat 10:20 "For it is not you who are speaking, but the Spirit of your Father speaking through you."

Mat 10:22 "And you will be hated by all for My name's sake, but he who perseveres and Endures to the end will be saved." **Mat 10:23** "When they persecute you in one town [*that is, pursue you in a manner that would injure you and cause you to suffer because of your belief*], flee to another town; for truly I tell you, you will not have gone through all the towns of Israel before the Son of Man comes."Why we are sometimes led by faith in God into something and you feel its right?
Everything seems to be working out perfectly, but in the end it does not work out (according to the plans you made!!)?

Heb 11:29 "By faith the people crossed the Red Sea as on dry land, but when the Egyptians tried to do the same thing they were swallowed up."

Heb 11:30 "Because of faith the walls of Jericho fell down after they had been encompassed for seven days."

Heb 11:36 "Others had to suffer the trial of mocking and scourging and even chains and imprisonment."

Heb 11:37 "They were stoned to death; they were lured with tempting offers; they were sawn asunder; they were slaughtered by the sword; they had to go about wrapped in the skins of sheep and goats, utterly destitute, oppressed, cruelly treated."

Heb 11:39 "And all of these, though they won divine approval by their faith, did not receive the fulfilment of what was promised."

Heb 11:40 "Because God had us in mind and had something better and greater in view for us, so that they [*these heroes and heroines of faith*] should not come to perfection apart from us." I have realized that God's plans are not my plans. He has His Glory in mind when He commands me to do something that might seem mad or senseless to others, and while I might be mocked or scorned by people for doing something foolish according to them, but I am obedient and do not fear the consequences of my actions, because His intention is for me to experience the fulfilment of all His promises and riches.

Revelation 32
God - The Accused

My friend Cobus visited me today. He came to reprimand me.

He said: „Andries, we must stop ACCUSING God! "

- We must stop throwing our fists in the air, accusing God for lack of finances or healings not breaking through, etc. We must stop murmuring like the Israelites in the desert – that's why some did not see the promised land. This is the same reason why we are not seeing lack changing into abundance and sickness turning into healing.

Job 34:37 You've compounded your original sin by rebelling against God's discipline, Defiantly shaking your fist at God, piling up indictments against the Almighty One."

Job 34:36 Job, you need to be pushed to the wall and called to account for wickedly talking back to God the way you have. My friend also said:

- We must refrain from accusing God; even if we have prayed and do not see any breakthrough.

- We must laugh at the lack in our houses, laugh at the sickness in our bodies, and laugh at what the devil throws at us. We must send out angels to get our abundance and healing.

- We must prophesy we have overflow and health.

- We must just praise God for abundance and healing already provided on the cross until it manifests.

I had a BIG issue with God, I accused Almighty God!

I said: „Lord, why do you provide for other people in abundance, but I sit in lack? I work for You but I am struggling to survive. Why don't You provide for me, like You provide for others not even serving You?
I looked at wealthy, unrighteous people and told myself: "I would probably never have abundance".
In this statement I actually ACCUSED God of providing better for the unrighteous than He does for me. I ACCUSED God of being a respecter of persons and a liar.

So today - I decided my life would change from now on. I decided I would learn not to accuse God:

- I decided that when I look at other people prospering, I would say: „Lord, I know that what You are doing for them by prospering them, You can do for me too and I bless those prosperous people with more in Jesus name.

- I decided to repent of my envy and praise God for my abundance.

- I decided I would not murmur over my circumstance, but rather praise God.

- I decided I would not accuse God by saying He is a liar when He says He is no respecter of the person. What He will do for one, He will do for the other.

•	I decided I would not focus on what other people have or buy and what I cannot buy, but focus on Jesus.

•	I decided I would just do my best in everything I do and leave the rest to God.

Mal 3:13 Your words have been strong and hard against Me, says the Lord. Yet you say what have we spoken against You?

Mal 3:14 You have said, It is useless to serve God, and what profit is it if we keep His ordinances and walk gloomily and as if in mourning apparel before the Lord of hosts?

Mal 3:15 And now we consider the proud and arrogant to be happy and favored; evildoers are Exalted and prosper; yes, and when they test God, they escape unpunished.

Mal 3:16 Then those who feared the Lord talked often one to another; and the Lord listened and heard it, and a book of remembrance was written before Him of those who reverenced and worshipfully feared the Lord and who thought on His name.

Mal 3:17 And they shall be Mine, says the Lord of hosts, in that day when I publicly recognize and openly declare them to be My jewels. And I will spare them, as a man spares his own son who serves him.

Mal 3:18 Then shall you return and discern between the righteous and the wicked, between him Who serves God and him who does not serve Him.

Revelation 33
A Covenant with God
According to the Historical
Blood River
Covenant

My friends Patrick, James and I, decided to take up a covenant with GOD, for our deteriorating condition in our businesses, ministries and finances to be changed.

We came together to discuss our current state of being – financially and spiritually. We were in real need and nothing seemed to work out for us. Because we know that we as Christians are supposed to reign on this earth, we realized that only with the help of God could the situation in our business, ministries and finances change.

We prayed earnestly for each of our situations. It's so easy to say to a person in need , „I will pray for you" and shift the responsibility to God to sort it out, but in the meantime God expects us to sort it out, because we are His hands and feet. We decided to sow a sacrificial seed into each other's lives.

We decided to make a **Covenant** with God on **9 December 2013** at the same place the **Blood River Covenant** memorial was erected.

***Covenant: Lord here we stand before You Holy God
of Heaven and Earth to take a Vow towards You
that if You will give us Breakthrough and Victory in
our businesses, ministries
and finances and change our lack into abundance
like You promised.***

*On this **9 December**, every year, we Andries, James
and*
Patrick will:

- ***Remember and Remind** each other of this day.*
- ***Pray** for each other in **Unity.***
- ***Use** our **Businesses, Ministries** and **Finances** to
  the Glory of Your Name.*
- ***Testify** to others of this day of **Breakthrough** and
  Victory in our businesses, ministries and the
  financial abundance You supplied. That this was
  only possible by You alone All Mighty God.*

***Signed on 9 December 2013 @ the Voortrekker
Monument BY:***

Father [God] Jesus Christ [Son] Holy Spirit

Andries Roux, Patrick Ellis, James Horn

From historical sources, it appears that the conditions
for the army deteriorated to such an extent that they
realized that they, only with the help of God, could
accomplish their task.

The Historical Blood River Covenant was first read on 9 December – 15 December 1838. Covenant: Here we stand before the Holy God of Heaven and Earth to do a Vow to Him that He will protect us and He will give our enemy into our hand. The day and date every year will be as a thanksgiving like a sabbatical upon them, and that a house in His honor will be raised up where He pleases , and that we teach our children to say that they have to share in the memory also for the future generations, for the glory of His name will be glorified by the fame and the glory of victory to Him .

On Saturday, 15 December, the scouts reported that the Zulus were close and pulled to a strategic location at the lower Ncome River. On Sunday, 16 December 1938, the Boers, accounting to 467 men, fought against a Zulu force of about 10000 men, a 20 to 1 ratio. This makes the Battle of Blood River the greatest military victory on South African soil; this River was called Blood River, because the blood of the slain Zulus turned the water red. It can be pointed out that it is considered impossible not to see **God's intervention** in these events.

All the Glory be to All Mighty God of Heaven and Earth

Revelation 34

Seek First the Kingdom of God – All will be Added

Why do we not see breakthroughs in our lives? Why are we struggling with lack of finances?
Why are we not getting healed?

It's because we are not in God's Kingdom.
I have been struggling to see any progress in my ministry and business. God said: „Seek first the Kingdom of God and all these things will be added unto you."

Mat 6:33 „But seek first of all His kingdom and His righteousness (His way of doing and being right), and then all these things taken together will be given you besides."

My conversation with God:

Andries: „Lord, what does seeking your Kingdom mean?
God: „Andries, seeking My Kingdom, does not mean going to church four days a week or reading and praying hours a day. That is a rule and a law. Seeking My Kingdom, does not even mean not sinning, because I already died and washed your sins away with My blood. Seeking My kingdom, is not giving tithes and offerings. The world seeks cars, money, fame, gold and silver. Andries, you don't have to seek

these things. You seek My Kingdom and all will be added. I said the gold and silver is
Mine and if you are in My kingdom, it's yours too."

Mat 6:32: „For the Gentiles (heathen) wish for and crave and diligently seek all these things, and your heavenly Father knows well that you need them all."

Hag 2:8: „ the silver is mine, and the gold is mine, said the
LORD of hosts."

Andries: „Lord, where is Your Kingdom?
God: My kingdom must be established from Heaven to here on earth, as it is said: let Your Kingdom come on earth as it is in heaven. My Kingdom is in your heart and in your mouth. Your body, mind and spirit is earth, My kingdom must be established on it."

Andries: „Lord, what is Your Kingdom?
God: Andries, My Kingdom is so easy to understand. My Kingdom is Righteousness, Peace and Joy.

Rom 14:17: „the kingdom of God is not a matter of food and drink, but instead it is righteousness (that state which makes a person acceptable to God) and peace and joy in the Holy Spirit."

Andries: „Lord, how do I seek Your Kingdom?
God: You must take action and exercise being righteous, being in total peace, even if things fall

apart around you. You must experience total joy, even if there is nothing to be joyful about."

Andries: „Lord, explain to me what does „God is righteousness" mean and what does „my righteousness" mean? **God:** My righteousness means, I am in a right relationship with you, I am not withholding any of my promises from you, I want you blessed in all areas of your life. Andries, your righteousness means, you are in the right relationship with Me, believing Me that I want you blessed and every promise fulfilled in your life."

Rom 14:18: „He who serves Christ in this way is acceptable and pleasing to God and is approved by men."

Andries:" Lord, what does peace mean?
God: Andries, My peace means not worrying about anything, because the world worries about stuff and is trying to get stuff; you don't have to, because if you believe and have peace, you will see My blessings."
When negative thoughts come, when fear come. Just resist and reject those thoughts. Nothing that instils fear comes from Me.

Mat 6:27: „And who of you by worrying and being anxious can add one unit of measure (cubit) to his stature or to the span of his life?"

Mat 6:28: „And why should you be anxious about clothes? Consider the lilies of the field and learn thoroughly how they grow; they neither toil nor spin."

Mat 6:31: „Therefore do not worry and be anxious, saying, what are we going to have to eat? Or, What are we going to have to drink? Or, What are we going to have to wear?"

Andries: „Lord, what does joy in the Holy Ghost mean? **God:** Andries, joy in the Holy Ghost means to laugh at you lack of finances or your sickness. You exercise having joy in bad circumstances and you will eventually see My blessings." **Mat 6:25:** „Therefore I tell you, stop being perpetually uneasy (anxious and worried) about your life, what you shall eat or what you shall drink; or about your body, what you shall put on. Is not life greater [in quality] than food, and the body [far above and more excellent] than clothing?"

Tips to follow:

•	When challenges come or something that disturbs me - being that finances or whatever – I just speak peace over it. I know God is righteous and I am righteous. I will not worry about this. Before I know that disturbing situation has changed into something good.

•	I vibrate God's presence with peace and joy in my heart; I keep this in mind all the time. And because of this, people are automatically attracted to me, because they see the peace and joy I vibrate.

•	Don't try to reason when calamity comes; don't think too much what is going to happen. Be led by Holy Spirit in righteousness, peace and joy.

•	Show some discipline by sticking to righteousness, peace and joy, even when it seems hard at first. I promise you if you exercise this and do what I am trying to tell you and grasp it, and do it for the next 30 days, your life will completely change and you will see miracles, breakthrough in finances, healing, etc.

Revelation 35
I have a GIFT for you

A) I recently sent an e-mail to my mailing list, saying:

A GIFT!!!

Hi to all you lovely people of God.
God our Father gave Jesus for us to abolish and pay for our sin on the cross. In this Passover we keep in remembrance this **GIFT** and sacrifice. NOW, House of Restoration also wants to give you a **GIFT** in this Passover time.

Our book: "Holy Book of Revelation" **A GIFT** for you - FREE!!!

All you have to do is reply to this e-mail and ASK FOR -
"Holy Book of Revelation- Life Changing Revelations" and we will mail you the LINK TO DOWNLOAD - FREEEEE!!! **End Result:** Just about 20 people of the more than 1600 people replied to my e-mail for the **FREE BOOK GIFT.**

B) I also recently blessed one of my friends, Jacque, with a Christian channel decoder. I sent this decoder to him via another friend. All he had to do was pick it up from this other friend.

End Result: Up to now Jacque has not picked up his
FREE
DECODER GIFT.

God said to me: "Andries, I have **given** you
everything in life to be successful, when Jesus said on
the cross: It's FINISHED! That was the day you
received everything in life. You don't have to ask for
things - you just have to receive them".

Joh 19:30 When Jesus had received the sour wine, He
said, It is finished! And He bowed His head and gave
up His spirit.

……The problem with **My** people is that I have **given**
them
GIFTS, but they don't RECEIVE, TAKE, and GET
the **GIFTS.** They keep on asking **Me over** and over
again for the same things, but I have already **given** it
to them – they must just RECEIVE, TAKE and GET
it.

I am not saying don't ask any more from God. I am
saying ask God in prayer for your healing, finances,
etc. and release that prayer in His hand, thanking Him
all the time for your healing, finances, etc., until it
manifests. Do not keep on asking for the same thing
over and over again. rather praise and thank Him over
and over again for what you have prayed for.

Mar 11:24 for this reason I am telling you, whatever
you ask

for in prayer, believe (trust and be confident)
that it is granted to you, and you will [*get it*].

Example: God **gave** us the spirit of self-control and
discipline
[**2Ti 1:7**]. We don't have to ask the Lord to **give** us
self-control and discipline over and over again. We
must thank God for it, receive it, take it and exercise
self-control.

See below what Paul did.

Act 24:16 Therefore I always exercise and discipline
myself [*mortifying my body, deadening my carnal
affections, bodily appetites, and worldly desires,
endeavoring in all respects*] to have a clear
conscience, void of offense toward God and toward
men.

1Co 9:27 But [*like a boxer*] I buffet my body [*handle
it roughly, discipline it by hardships*] and subdue it,
for fear that after proclaiming to others the Gospel
and things pertaining to it, I myself should become
unfit [*not stand the test, be unapproved and rejected
as a counterfeit*].
Gal 6:16 Peace and mercy be upon all who walk by
this rule
[*who discipline themselves and regulate their
lives by this principle*], even upon the [*true*]
Israel of God!
2Ti 1:7 For God did not **give** us a spirit of timidity (of
cowardice, of craven and cringing and

fawning fear), but [He has **given** us a spirit] of power and of love and of calm and well balanced

Note: Please if you fail RECEIVING these **GIFTS** from God, don't judge yourself. Just stand up and grow into receiving these **GIFTS. Look at all th**ese **examples in the scriptures of what God has already GIVEN us:**

Rom 6:23 For the wages which sin pays is death, but the **free**
gift of God is eternal life
through Jesus Christ our
Lord.
Joh 1:12 But to as many as did receive and welcome Him, He **gave** the authority (power, privilege, right) to become the children of God, that is, to those who believe in His name.
Ps 127:2 It is vain for you to rise up early, to take rest late, to eat the bread of toil--for He **gives** [*blessings*] to His beloved in sleep.
Pro 3:34 Though He scoffs at the scoffers and scorns the scorners, yet He **gives** His undeserved favor to the low, the humble, and the afflicted.
Ecc 2:26 For to the person who pleases Him God **gives** wisdom and knowledge and joy; but to the sinner He **gives** the work of gathering and heaping up, that he may **give** to one who pleases God. This also is vanity and a striving after the wind and a feeding on it.
Isa 40:29 He **gives** power to the faint and weary, and to him who has no might He increases strength.

Jos 6:2 And the Lord said to Joshua, See, I have **given** Jericho, its king and mighty men of valor, into your hands.

 Jos 1:3 Every place upon which the sole of your foot shall tread, that have I **given** to you, as I promised Moses

 Joh 17:2 You have granted Him power and authority over all flesh, so that He may **give** eternal life to all whom You have **given** Him.

Joh 10:28 And I **give** them eternal life, and they shall never lose it or perish throughout the ages. And no one is able to snatch them out of My hand.

Joh 4:14 But whoever takes a drink of the water that I will **give** him shall never, no never, be thirsty any more. But the water that I will **give** him shall become a spring of water welling up within him unto eternal life.

Joh 5:21 Just as the Father raises up the dead and **gives** them life, even so the Son also **gives** life to whomever He wills and is pleased to **give** it.

Joh 1:12 But to as many as did receive and welcome Him, He **gave** the authority to become the children of God, that is, to those who believe in His name.

Joh 6:31 Our forefathers ate the manna in the wilderness; as the Scripture says, He **gave** them bread out of heaven to eat. **1Co 7:7** I wish that all men were like I myself am. But each has his own special **gift** from God, one of this kind and one of another.

Eph 1:3 May blessing be to the God and Father of our Lord Jesus Christ Who has **blessed** us in Christ with every spiritual **blessing** in the heavenly realm!

Heb 2:8 For You have put everything in subjection under his feet. Now in putting everything in subjection to man, **He left nothing outside [*of man's*] control.** But at present we do not yet see all things subjected to him.

1Co 6:19 Do you not know that your body is the temple of the Holy Spirit Who lives within you, whom you have received [*as a **Gift***] from God? You are not your own.

Rom 11:29 For God's **gifts** and His call are irrevocable. That is why He says, God sets Himself against the proud and haughty, but **gives** grace to the lowly (those who are humble enough to receive it).

Isa 53:5 But He was wounded for our transgressions, He was bruised for our guilt and iniquities; the chastisement peace and well-being for us was upon Him, and with the stripes Him **we are healed** and made whole.

2Pe 1:3 For His divine power has **bestowed upon** us all things that to life and godliness, through the knowledge of Him Who called us by and to His own glory and excellence (virtue).

Foot note: AGAIN!!! …The issue is not that God do not listen or **give** to us, the problem is that we don't let ourselves receive the **gifts** from God.

Revelation 36
Respect works "Down" not "Up"

I started working in April 2012 as a branch manager for a big company a few years ago. The first few weeks everything was good and I learned a lot from the outgoing manager. I then started seeing some cracks in the way the company treated their workers. The workers were upset by the way they were treated, shouted and sworn at.

One issue I addressed was that one of our maintenance guys had to drive at his own expense to call-outs at the plant. On another occasion the engineer hit one guy behind the head, because he gave a wrong answer to a question in a meeting.

These practices really upset me and I addressed these issues with my direct boss forcefully. The following day the COO of the company accused me of not "showing respect" to my superior, they charged me with "gross subordination".

I was very upset. I asked God to help me understand. I stood up for people under me, I stood up for stuff that was wrong and I was charged because of it.

God said this: Respect works **"DOWN"** not **"UP"**. Show respect downwards first. People in managerial positions in life or business or any other area will always say that people in inferior positions must show them respect, but God says NO! This is not the way. People in managerial positions have to show respect FIRST to the people in lower positions. People in lower positions will gladly follow and give managers the highest respect if the managers show them respect first.

Example: Jesus showed us His love and respect FIRST by dying for our sin on the cross.

Joh 3:16 For God so greatly loved and dearly prized the world that He gave up His only begotten Son, so that whoever believes in (trusts in, clings to, relies on) Him shall not perish but have eternal (everlasting) life.
Joh 3:17 For God did not send the Son into the world in order to judge (to reject, to condemn, to pass sentence on) the world, but that the world might find salvation and be made safe and sound through Him.

Example: David showed his 3 mighty men respect first. When David said he was thirsty for a drink of water, these 3 mighty men went into the enemy's camp and got him a drink of water from the well. Out of respect for what these 3 mighty men did, he declined the drink of water.

2Sa 23:15 And David said longingly, Oh, that someone would give me a drink of water from the well of Bethlehem by the gate!
2Sa 23:16 And the three mighty men broke through the army of the Philistines and drew water out of the

well of Bethlehem by the gate and brought it to
David. But he would not drink it, but poured it out to
the Lord.
2Sa 23:17 And he said, Be it far from me, O Lord, to
drink this. Is it not the blood of the men who went at
the risk of their lives? So he would not drink it. These
things did the three mighty men.

Husbands, do you want your wives to respect you?
Be a man of character, not a wimp, and stand up for
what is right and love your wife unconditionally.
Parents, do you want your children to respect you?
Do not spoil them, give them discipline and love.
Pastors, do you want your congregation to respect
you? Show them the love of Jesus, pray for them.
Employers, do you want your employees to respect
you? Treat them fairly and with dignity.
Employees, do you want your boss to respect you?
Show them respect first by showing sincerity and
genuine interest in their lives.
Teachers, do you want your pupils to respect you?
Respect them by listening to their opinions.
School youth leaders, do you want the lower grade
pupils to respect you? Respect them first by being
interested in them as persons.
Young girls in love, do you want your boyfriends to
respect you? Don't give him sex before marriage.
Friends, do you want your friends to respect you?
Stop talking about your problems and issues and start
listening to their problems and issues.

Respect people first any they will respect you for a lifetime.

Heb 7:7 In acts of blessing, the lesser is blessed by the greater. **Note:** I was asked to leave the company after just one month, but because of me standing up for what is right the maintenance guy receives compensation for call-outs to the plant.

COMING SOON:

MORE

REVELATIONS

WILL

BE

ADDED

Contact Details:

andriesroux77@gmail.com